Building in the USSR 1917–1932

Building in the USSR 1917–1932

Edited by O. A. Shvidkovsky

Studio Vista London

Acknowledgements

Various people have helped to make the publication of this collection of essays possible and the publishers would like to thank first the editors of *Architectural Design* magazine, Monica Pidgeon and Robin Middleton, for assembling and editing the bulk of the text and illustrations. As was admitted in their introduction there were only two outstanding lacunae in an otherwise comprehensive coverage of the major Russian constructivist architects, articles on Melnikov and the Vesnin brothers. We have remedied this situation by the inclusion of two recent articles from *Arkhitektura*; these were translated by John Milner, who should also be thanked for editing this new collection on behalf of the publishers and for providing the valuable bibliography. The original articles have thus been through many hands and because of the limitations of space have had in some cases to be compressed. However, we hope that the results will be of value in increasing knowledge and understanding of a most interesting period of architectural history.

This collection © in translation Studio Vista 1971
Blue Star House, Highgate Hill, London N19
Chapters 1–5 and 8–16 first published in translation
by *Architectural Design* London 1970, published by Studio Vista 1971
Chapters 6 and 7 first published in translation by Studio Vista 1971
Set in 11 pt Plantin 2 pt leaded
Printed and bound
by The Whitefriars Press Ltd London and Tonbridge

SBN 289 70144 9

Contents

Notes on contributors

Barkhin, Mikhail Grigorovich: born 1906, studied at the Moscow Institute of Structural Engineers, finishing in 1929, supervised by L. Vesnin. He worked first for his architectural professor, Pantelemon Golosov, then, after 1924, for his father G. B. Barkhin. He has built many housing and industrial estates. Has taught since 1929, first at Moscow Institute of Architecture, then at the Academy of Engineering. In 1956 became Professor of Planning. Now chief researcher in the Institute of Art History.

Beloussov, Vladimir Nikolaevich: born Moscow 1928, completed studies at the Moscow School of Architecture in 1950. Worked for L. Rudniev. Since 1957 has taught at Moscow School of Architecture. In 1968 he visited England.

Khan-Mahomedov, Selim Omarovich: born 1928, completed studies at Moscow School of Architecture in 1951, doctoral thesis submitted 1968. From 1949 onwards worked on the history of architecture in Daghestan then, from 1955, on the architecture of the USSR 1917–32. Editor of Vol. X of the *General History of Architecture*.

Khazanova, V: born 1924, Moscow, studied at the Moscow State University. Researcher in the Institute of Art History, Ministry of Culture. Her main works are *The History of Soviet architecture*: I 1917–25, Moscow 1963, II 1926–32, Moscow 1970.

Kyrilov, Vladimir Vasilievich: born Moscow 1925, studied at the Moscow Polytechnic and then at the State University. Has taught at the State University for ten years, specializing in the history of Russian architecture; author of a *History of Soviet Architecture in the* 1920s, Moscow University Press, 1970.

Shvidkovsky, Oleg Alexandrovich: born 1925, studied at Moscow School of Architecture then at the Institute of Town Planning. Since 1947 has studied architectural history and has published numerous articles and books, in particular *Town planning in Czechoslovakia*. Has contributed to the *General history of art* and the *History of Russian Art*. Since 1968 has been deputy director of the Institute of Art History.

Creative trends 1917-1932

S. O. Khan-Mahomedov

1

2

3

1 Red Star, propaganda ship, 1926
2 Agit train 'Lenin', 1919, cinema coach
3 Agit train, 1919

Soviet architecture – the first truly socialist architecture – emerged during a period of tremendous upheaval. The years of dynamic regeneration were from 1917 to 1930, when a relatively small number of architects developed an architecture that had worldwide influence.

Immediately after the Revolution and the civil war – with the consequent collapse of the country's economy – there was very little new building. But, even during these years, Soviet architects wished to create a new form of architecture, free from conservative Tsarist traditions.

The first state schools of architecture were opened in Moscow and Petrograd, and several architectural societies resumed activity – the Moscow Architectural Society (MAO – chairman, A. V Shchusev), the Petrograd Society of Architects (POA, later LOA – chairman, V. Evald) and the Society of Painters and Architects in Petrograd (OAKh – chairman, L. N. Benoit). They were mostly intent on reviving the old architectural traditions. Their membership was largely made up of established architects.

But even in the early years, amid the quarrels of the eclectics and the conservatives, a new spirit was evident. There were strong links between architects and the members of left-wing art movements formed before the first world war.

Throughout Europe there was a similar crystallization between the fine arts and a revitalized architecture. Architecture, which for long had ceded its primacy to painting was slowly recovering its traditional lead. But the process of renewal was first evident in experimental painting – Cubism, Suprematism, Neo-plasticism – which not only purified the traditional art of painting, but was based on forms and techniques that were outside the range of painting as it was previously understood. Architecture found a new stimulus in such innovations. Throughout Europe the younger architects were allied to painters and derived inspiration from them – in Holland there were the members of De Stijl, in Germany the Bauhaus, and the international currents of Art Nouveau had brought the arts closer together earlier in the century. In Russia, things were no different, institutions and organizations such as UNOVIS, VKHUTEMAS, INKHUK, ZHIVSKULPTARKH (a contraction of the Russian words for painting, sculpture and architecture) were formed.

During this period of interaction the work of Malevich, of Tatlin, of El Lissitzky and A. Vesnin was of the greatest significance for the future of Soviet architecture. Irrespective of their training, these men worked as painters, as architects and designers, as book illustrators and stage designers. The complexity and variety of their work, however, was not only due to their multifarious talents, but was also a response to newly formulated attitudes and ideals.

Kasimir Malevich's 'Arkhitektoniks', Vladimir Tatlin's 'Counter-reliefs', El Lissitzky's 'Prouns' and Aleksandr Vesnin's stage designs all enabled architects to assimilate the new aesthetic discoveries of the painters. These ceased to be limited to the representation of objects, and were applied instead to their construction.

Malevich, like Mondrian, pursued a course in painting that led directly to architecture. His experiments tended to destroy barriers between painting and architecture.

As an architect, El Lissitzky was one of the first to sense the importance for architecture of Malevich's experiments. Working both as a painter and architect, he was able to make apparent to architects the newest discoveries. His 'Prouns' formed a symbiosis between painting and architecture – a prerequisite of the new socialist architecture. All upholders of the new art forms were active at this period. They were involved together in the organization of festivals, demonstrations and public gatherings. They designed murals, posters, placards and slogans. Art, in a literal sense, moved into the streets, reflecting the activities of the people.

'Streets are our brushes, squares our palettes,' proclaimed Mayakovsky. He himself helped to decorate streets, to design propaganda trains and produce open-air plays. A. Vesnin, A. Rodchenko, V. Tatlin, K. Malevich, N. Gabo, V. Stepanova, L. Popova, El Lissitzky, A. Khan, D. Sternberg, K. Petrov-Vodkin, N. Dobuzhinsky, A. Lentulov and I. Nivinsky were all similarly involved.

N. Altman designed the festival decorations for Palace Square in Petrograd; Marc Chagall, artistic commissar in Vitebsk, decorated the streets and squares of that town.

Such propaganda art, which usually involved small architectural elements – tribunes, kiosks, etc. – and was often designed by architects, could not fail to influence the course of architecture.

4

5

6   7

4 Open air tableau, 'The storming of the Winter Palace', designer Y. Annenkov, director N. Evreinov, 1919

5 A model of Tatlin's tower drawn through the streets of Leningrad

6, 7 Conducting a concert for factory sirens, c. 1920, an artistic form first proposed by the poets Gastev and Mayakovsky

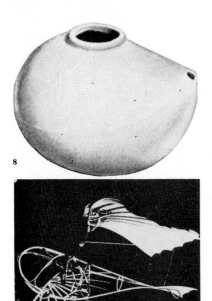

8

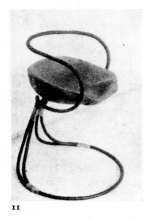

9

10

11

8 Tatlin: teapot

9 Tatlin: flying machine 'Letatlin', 1931

10 Tatlin: corner relief, suspended type. Collation of materials, iron, aluminium, primer, 1915

11 Tatlin: chair, *c.* 1927

The most famous of these early manifestations was Vladimir Tatlin's design of 1919 of a memorial tower to the Third International. This project, romantically symbolic, richly appealing, provided the vital visual inspiration for architects seeking to give form to both their new artistic tenets and their structural ideals. It is, in its way, as significant as Eiffel's tower.

All artists were united by the desire to provide adequate working and leisure environments for workers in the new state. The VKHUTEMAS studios which combined in one institution faculties of architecture, production and art, were established in Moscow at the end of 1920 with this prime aim. Such leading architectural figures as Melnikov, N. Ladovsky, A. and L. Vesnin, I. and P. Golosov, M. Ginsburg and V. Krinsky lectured there.

Discussion was fierce, experiments daring and innovation intrepid. Many new ideas were to emerge. But the path of development was by no means uniform; there were two main trends, one towards Rationalism, the other towards Constructivism. The two centres in which the ideas of these movements were first formulated were VKHUTEMAS and INKHUK (Institute of Artistic Culture), both founded in the same year.

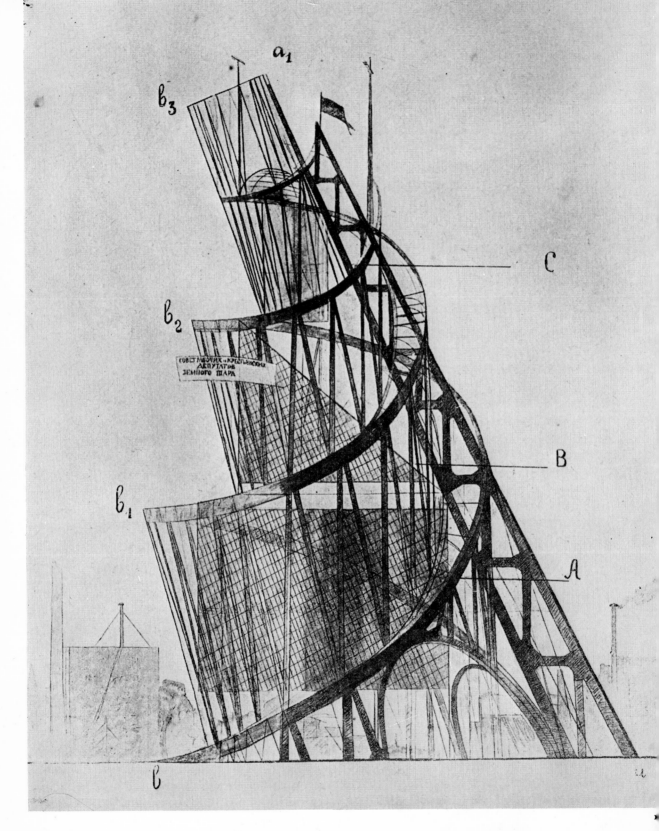

12 Drawing of Vladimir Tatlin's monument to the Third International reproduced in N. N. Punin's pamphlet, 1920

13 Poster for the film *Battleship Potemkin*, 1926

14 Aleksei Gan: propaganda kiosk, 1923

INKHUK included such painters as A. Babichev, A. Rodchenko, L. Popova and V. Stepanova, and the theorists B. Arbatov, A. Kushner and O. Brik who together influenced the ideas of the two leaders of the movements – N. A. Ladovsky (Rationalism), and A. Vesnin (Constructivism).

Ladovsky's followers banded together first in 1919 at the painters, sculptors and architects' union (ZHIVSKULPTARKH), then, after 1920, in an independent group. In 1921 they joined the architects of the Institute of Artistic Culture (INKHUK) which, in 1923, became the Association of New Architects (ASNOVA). The founder members of ASNOVA were N. Dokuchaev, V. Krinsky, A. Rukhlyadev, A. Efimov, V. Friedman and I. Mochalov. Melnikov was also a member. Ladovsky was the President.

The Rationalists were determined to evolve new artistic forms, making use of new building materials and techniques; emphasis was laid on the rational expression of structure. But they went further. A programme drawn up in 1921 by a committee of architects from INKHUK, constituting the first theoretical document of Rationalism, demanded that particular attention be paid to the understanding of space. These architects hoped that objective criteria for the perception of space and form might be established and buildings designed in accordance with them.

The Constructivists were more concerned with the heightened expression of structure as an end in itself. In 1922 A. Vesnin expounded his personal credo at INKHUK, thus laying down the first principles of architectural Constructivism. 'Things created by modern artists', he said, 'must be pure constructions, devoid of the ballast of representation . . .'

In its early stages, the architectural Constructivist movement was under the influence of artistic Constructivism, a dominant movement in Russia in the 1920s, concerned with the creation of a mass-produced art for the people. In August 1920 the 'Realist Manifesto' of the brothers Naum Gabo and Anton Pevsner was issued. A working group of Constructivists was formed in INKHUK in March 1921; among the members were A. Khan, A. Rodchenko, V. Stepanova and V. and G. Stenberg.

The views of these Constructivist artists approximated more closely to Vesnin's than to those of the architects who joined the committee of INKHUK architects headed by N. Ladovsky. An architectural group gradually formed round Vesnin, composed mainly of VKHUTEMAS students – M. Barshch, A. Burov, I Sobolev, L. Komarova, N. Krassilnikov – to whom were allied a

number of prominent members of the LEF (Leftist Art Front) led by
V. Mayakovsky, O. Brik and A. Lavinsky.

In the Stroganov College and other pre-Revolutionary schools of
art, methods of teaching were based on the acquisition of a craft,
but at VKHUTEMAS the Constructivists aimed at new rational
principles of design and manufacture that would result in the mass
production of objects that were both beautiful and useful – folding
beds, furniture, stoves, kitchen utensils and clothing. They were
concerned with the efficient and economical production of con-
sumer goods. This was Aleksandr Vesnin's prime concern and it was
this aspect of his thought that was taken up by the architects who
joined together to form the Constructivist group. They wanted a
modern, functional architecture, furnished with mass-produced
goods.

Architectural Constructivism was first given form early in 1923,
in the competition design for the Palace of Labour by the Vesnin
brothers. The significance of this project lay in the fact that social
meaning was given to a public building through the convincing
use of new and functional architectural forms. The brothers were at
once acclaimed leaders of Constructivism. But the propaganda for
the movement was provided by M. Ginsburg. In polemical articles
in the magazine *Architecture** (1923), and in his book *Style and
Epoch* (1924), he analysed the evolution of the new forms, stressing
their technical basis. He strongly upheld what he called 'the
mechanization of life' – the integration of scientific and technical
discoveries into the process of rational artistic creation.

The aesthetic and formal explorations of these years determined
to a considerable degree the development of Soviet architecture.
But formal problems were by no means adequately resolved; both
the relationship between form and functional and structural
requirements, and that between form and all verifiable principles
of perception, remained in doubt. These were the subjects of
particular Rationalist and Constructivist study – and contention.
But though the two parties diverged in their interpretations, they
were, ultimately, complementary in their approach.

By the mid-twenties, when building was being seriously under-
taken, aesthetic considerations gave way to a more realistic apprecia-
tion of the social effects of architecture.

At the end of 1925 the Constructivists, merging the original LEF
architectural group and a band of architects headed by A. Nikolsky
in Leningrad, formed a society of their own, OSA (Union of Con-

* *Arkhitektura* in the Russian

15 A. Rodchenko: design for a worker's
club, 1925
16 A. Rodchenko: poster for Vertov's 'Kino
Glaz' (Cinema Eye), Moscow 1925
17 A. Rodchenko: cover of the magazine
LEF, 1923

18

19

18 A. Rodchenko: architectural project, 1920

19 A. Rodchenko and his wife Stepanova, 1920

temporary Architects). Among the architects were the Vesnin brothers, M. Barshch, A. Burov, G. Bergman, V. Vladimirov, M. Ginsburg, I. Golosov, I. Leonidov, I. Nikolaev, A. Nikolsky, N. Krassilnikov, G. Orlov, A. Pasternak, N. Sokolov, I. Sobolev, R. Khiger, F. Yalovkin; the engineers included A. Lolleit and G. Karlsen; A. Khan joined as a craftsman. Aleksandr Vesnin was chairman and together with Ginsburg acted as editor of the OSA journal, *Contemporary Architecture (Sovremennaya Arkhitektura)*.

But the supremacy of both the Constructivists and the Rationalists in the architectural world was ensured not so much by their establishment as strong and independent artistic bodies, as through their outstanding successes in a series of architectural competitions held in 1924 and 1925 – a headquarters in Moscow for *Pravda* (projects submitted by K. Melnikov, the Vesnins and I. Golosov); the Arcos building (projects by the Vesnins, K. Melnikov and V. Krinsky); the Soviet pavilion for the Paris Exhibition of 1925 (K. Melnikov, N. Ladovsky and M. Ginsburg); the textile building (I. Golosov and M. Ginsburg); the Moscow Telegraph building (A. Shchusev and the Vesnins); the State Trade building in Kharkov (S. Serafimova and A. Dmitriev). These demonstrable successes attracted considerable attention and as a result many architects adopted a 'Constructivist' style.

The Constructivists themselves were greatly alarmed. They foresaw that their innovations might lead to nothing more than stylistic application. They started a campaign against 'style' as such. Their attacks together with their justifications for their own position were printed in their journal *Contemporary Architecture* between 1926 and 1930.

They laid most stress on 'functionalism' as the means of avoiding stylistic excess. Ginsburg wrote most of the justificatory articles. Functionalism was, in fact, the basic creed of all advanced architecture in Russia at this period. By it was understood the integration of rational principles of planning with advanced building techniques. Functionalists – and the Constructivists in particular – stood for standardization, the industrializing of the building industry, the introduction of assembly line principles and prefabrication. Overenthusiastic in their faith in technology, they exaggerated, perhaps, the possibilities of rationalized methods of construction. But, at the time, their faith seemed justified. However, a synthesis of both the Constructivist and Rationalist tenets seemed more than ever necessary in the second half of the 1920s, when building activity had greatly increased and stylistic variations of their innovatory

designs were being applied indiscriminately by unscrupulous
architects to the most boring and *retardataire* plans and compositions. Two architects, in particular, attempted to resolve the
Constructivist/Rationalist dilemma – Melnikov and Leonidov. They
sought to give convincing and satisfying form to the newly formulated ideals.

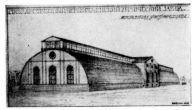

20

Melnikov, one of the most imaginative architects of the twentieth
century, provided a range of new formal solutions, starting with his
Soviet pavilion in Paris in 1925, continuing with his famous
workers' clubs. He invariably devised new planning solutions and
gave to them direct and dramatic expression in the massing of his
forms. Leonidov, a combination of painter, inventor, and theorist,
was equally concerned to give expressive geometric form to his
compositions, but he simplified where Melnikov composed and
complicated. He broke his buildings down into isolated and independent geometric units. The forms were all simple and powerful.
Aleksandr Vesnin regarded his project for the Lenin Institute,
shown at the Exhibition of Contemporary Architecture in Moscow
in 1927, as the starting point for the new architecture.

21

A. Nikolsky, leader of the Leningrad Constructivist group,
pursued another independent course, composing with interlocking
vertical and horizontal elements, all highly coloured.

As the new movement gained in strength, older architects such
as A. V. Shchusev sought to adjust themselves to it. Shchusev's
Telegraph building in Moscow, completed in 1925, is an example
of the new, stripped classicism; while in the Lenin mausoleum, set
up as a permanent structure in 1930, he did away with all classical
detailing, making it a simple geometric composition. Even I.
Fomin, one of the principal protagonists of Russian classicism,
attempted a compromise. He evolved the so-called 'Red Doric'
style, which consisted of applying attenuated and usually paired
columns (without capitals or entasis) to a modern structural
framework. Other established architects were more recalcitrant:
I. Zholtovsky and A. Tamanyan held steadfastly to a traditional
course and were rewarded when they emerged triumphant after
1933, strongly influencing the course of Russian architecture up
to 1954. Zholtovsky was a great connoisseur of the Italian Renaissance and was quite consistent in his belief that this was the source
of all excellence in architecture. Tamanian, less strict, combined
classical with traditional Armenian forms, and was more adept at
this than other upholders of architectural 'nationalism'.

The real contribution of the 1920s, however, came from the

22

20 V. A. Vesnin: design for the
Chernovechensky super-phosphate works,
1920

21 Vesnin Brothers: design for a chemical
factory on the Vakhtan, 1924

22 I. V. Zholtovsky: office building in
Moscow, 1934, now the headquarters of
Intourist

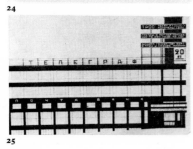

23 A. A. and L. A. Vesnin: design for Telegraph building, Moscow

24 V. A. Vesnin: design for a turpentine plant on the Vakhtan, 1922

25 A. Shchusev: project for Telegraph building, Kharkov, 1927

Rationalists – N. Ladovsky, K. Melnikov, El Lissitzky, V. Krinsky, V. Balikhin, A. Korzhev, etc. – and the Constructivists – A. and V. Vesnin, M. Ginsburg, I. Leonidov, A. Nikolsky, P. and I. Golosov, V. Vladimirov, A. Burov, M. Barshch, etc. Their work was of the greatest influence not only in Russia, but also abroad, being published in numerous magazines. But the interminable quarrels of such innovators and their increasingly theoretical postulations were destructive of the architectural cohesion and coherence that were needed once building began in earnest, and, in particular when the first of the five-year plans, implementing larger-scale development than had ever been dreamed of, was initiated in 1928. The strife in architectural circles was already regarded as a force of disruption. Early in 1928, the Council of OSA (A. Vesnin, M. Ginsburg, I. Leonidov, R. Rochter and G. Orlov) proposed that all the independent groups be united, to provide a focus for the renewal of all Soviet architecture. This proved impractical. Dissension was, indeed, further increased by the formation, early in 1929, of the 'All-Russia Union of Proletarian Architects (VOPRA) among whose founder-members were K. Alabyan V. Baburov A. Vlasov, K. Ivanov, G. Kochar, M. Mazmanyan, I. Matsa, N. Poliakov and V. Simbirtsev. They vilified all other groups, concentrating in particular on those architects who were most experimental. 'Leonidovism' became a special term of abuse. Idealism and abstract theorizing were replaced by crude power politics and an unjustifiably high estimation of the works of the members, of VOPRA.

Some of VOPRA's criticism was not without foundation but the effect of the attack was to lead architectural discussion into an ever more rarefied sphere of formulations and definitions. VOPRA claimed, above all, that the young leaders were, despite all evidence to the contrary, 'non-proletarian'.

The unrest thus stimulated prepared the way for the return of the traditionalists, for the members of VOPRA themselves had nothing to offer. The successive stages of the competition for the Palace of the Soviets held in the early 1930s made this increasingly evident. The forms of the early modernists were gradually replaced by a dull, lack-lustre stylization, tending towards archaic monumentality. An effort was made to counteract the pressure of the VOPRA attack. In May 1930 the 'All Union Scientific Architectural Society' (VANO) was formed to co-ordinate most of the earlier groups. The Moscow branch (MOVANO) was made up of ASNOVA, OSA (which had become SASS) and ARU, each of which nonetheless retained some indepen-

26 Tatlin standing in front of a home-made oven; models of clothes sewn by himself; and Tatlin wearing jacket and suit

dence. But the process of amalgamation was slow, and VOPRA, which had remained militantly independent, was able to attack with impunity – in much the same way as RAPP conducted its campaign against the more advanced literary groups at this time. The party was compelled to intervene to prevent such strife. In a decree of 23 April 1932 – 'Reform of literary and artistic bodies' – all such groups were dissolved. In July 1932, the Union of Soviet Architects was formed with members of the earlier societies elected to its committee – K. Alabyan, V. Balikhin, M. Ginsburg, I. Zholtovsky, N. Ladovsky and others.

(translation Marina Corby)

Soviet Architectural Associations 1917-1932*

V. Khazanova

The eight months between the February and the great October socialist revolutions were notable in Russian architectural life for numerous remarkable events. Large meetings of building and construction workers were called to meet engineers and architects. Appeals were written, proclaiming the beginning of a new era.

'The long awaited moment has come ... Despotism, based on blood, darkness and the helplessness of the people is overthrown by the revolutionary proletariat and the revolutionary army. The nests of the old régime are burnt ... A new life is coming ... We must create a new order for ourselves. It is essential to establish a new organization for all builders, without exception.' It was with words such as these that on Saturday, 4 March 1917, the working comrades of the organized building workers in Petrograd were informed of a general town meeting. Five days later, on Thursday 9 March, the representatives of more than forty artistic organizations from Petrograd were gathered together at the invitation of the Association of Architects of the Academy of Fine Arts. On Sunday, 12 March, at the Mikhailovsky Theatre, the second gathering of leaders of all branches of the arts took place. Presiding were A. Benoit, M. Gorky, A. Glazunov, the architect M. Lalevich and others. A. Tamanyan delivered a speech full of civic verve, dismissing the old bureaucracy and opening the way to a new life.

Architects enthusiastically set to work. A competition was announced for the execution of a monument to the victims of the Revolution. It was the first commission from the state. M. Gorky, A. Lunacharsky and A. Blok headed the first jury and selected the project of L. Rudnev. The work was completed in 1920 and is an outstanding example of Soviet architecture.

MAO

When the Soviet Government moved to Moscow, in 1918, the architects re-formed their association. It was known as MAO – the

* See appendix on page 132 for further details of Soviet architectural associations and their activities.

Moscow Association of Architects. It was originally headed by
Shekhtel'* and from 1922 by Shchusev. One of their aims was to
protect and consolidate their newly acquired freedom, to legislate
for building and organize training. The other was to serve the
people and put an end to exploitation.

Soon after this, a plan was initiated in Moscow to amalgamate all
associations, but this was only achieved much later. Nevertheless,
Leningrad collaborated in carrying out Lenin's monumental plan
of propaganda. Norberg, Chernyshev, Ladovsky, Osipov, Vsavol-
sky, Efimov, Vasiliev, Dokuchaev, the Vesnin brothers, Kokorin
and Kolli competed for the design for a monument for the Soviet
constitution and other sculptural embellishments. The *Sovnarkom*
published decrees on 9 May and 18 June 1918 for the administration of VSNKh† and proceedings and regulations for building and
planning. Many meetings and regular conferences were organized.
The first All-Russia conference for productivity and building took
place in 1923. By 1925 the delegates included Shchusev, Malinovsky,
Semenov, Ginsburg and others. The Petrograd association worked
on the Petrosoviet building under I. Fomin and jointly with MAO
on planning and cultural projects.

Many members of MAO took part in the preservation work of
various associations such as 'Old Moscow', 'The Association for the
Study of the Moscow Province', etc.

In 1922 they launched architectural competitions. In 1924
Lunacharsky organized one for the construction of Lenin's mausoleum. They planned dwellings for workers, a garden city (1922), a
communal house in Ivano-Voznessensk (1925), a Palace of Work
in Rostov-on-Don, a workers' club in Briansk, public buildings,
such as banks, in Moscow (Arcos‡), Novosibirsk, and Sverdlovsk,
post offices, a university in Minsk, the Republican Hospital in
Samarkand, a monument to Karl Marx and the 1923 Exhibition.

LOA and OAKh

In Leningrad, there were two groups of architects – LOA (The
Leningrad Association of Architects) presided over by L. Benoit
and OAKh (The Association of Architects and Painters). Both were
engaged on similar work to MAO. They concentrated on factory
building, housing estates and competitions. The organization of

* Editor's note: Shekhtel' was an exponent of Russian Art Nouveau and Arts
and Crafts Movement.
  † Editor's note: VSNKh: an abbreviation for the Higher Soviet of National Owner-
ship.
  ‡ Editor's note: Arcos: an abbreviation for the Anglo-Soviet Trade Organization.

courses began in 1924 and the first 280 students graduated in 1928. In 1924 they also reissued the journal *The Architect*. Their immediate concern was the relationship between art and architecture. They sponsored a new association 'Old Petersburg – New Leningrad' and made themselves responsible for the protection of old monuments. Notable competitions were organized, such as projects for the Pushkin monument, the Botkin memorial hospital, the concert hall in Sverdlovsk, the Leningrad Palace of Culture and a zoo. Prices were awarded for the Lenin monument in Leningrad and the House of Productivity in Kharkov. Extensive work was done on the planning of houses and clubs for workers (Leningrad – Murmansk). *Annual* (1927–30) reported their activities regularly.

It is now apparent that there were many dissensions between the Moscow and Leningrad associations in their attitudes towards Soviet architecture. Leningrad did not always approve of Moscow's new conception of architecture and considered Moscow architects enslaved to the ideas of the Western world. In 1927, most of their members refused to take part in a competition organized by the MAO. Only problems of creativity provided a common ground.

ASNOVA

In 1923 N. Ladovsky, professor at VKHUTEMAS, together with Dokuchaev and Krinsky, organized the 'New Association of Architects' which conveniently abbreviates into ASNOVA, meaning foundation. They advocated a synthesis of architecture, painting and sculpture. Work was to be carried out by a collective body using new machinery, new methods and new terminology. There had to be a collaboration between producers (the architects) and consumers (the working masses). They introduced the use of 'psycho-analytical' methods in the study of architecture and the influence of shapes on man. The extent of their work was, at first, limited and they refused to take part in competitions. Their activities were reported in many publications, *Architecture of the* VKHUTEMAS, *Moscow Construction, Industry of Building, From Art to Masses* as well as their own journal, *News from* ASNOVA, which started in 1926. Some change occurred in the late twenties and they took part in competitions, organized exhibitions and received commissions. In 1921 they clarified their position and defined architecture as proletarian and a combination of plasticity of form and functionalism. Architecture, they held, should be linked with nature.

Towards the end of the twenties, the merits of the new methods became apparent and ASNOVA participated in competitions. Their 'collective brigades' planned a theatre in Kharkov, the Palace of the Soviets in Moscow (architects – Balikhin, Budo, Prokhorov, Turkus; sculptor – Iodko; decorator – Sevortyan) and many other buildings. Some of their theories did not work out, but their formulation of a collective creative method still attracts attention.

ARU

In 1928 Ladovsky and a few other members left ASNOVA which they considered too involved in abstract theory. They formed the Association of Urban Architects, ARU, in order to concentrate on planning methods essential to the reconstruction of the state and particularly the development of nationalized land. They considered architecture as a socialist and psychological means of educating the masses. They advocated courses in urbanism and the popularization of their aims. Projects were carried out by Ladovsky and students of VKHUTEMAS (a theatre in Sverdlovsk, a housing estate for the Telbesk factory, Trubnoy Square in Moscow and plans for the development of middle Asia).

OSA

One of the most popular associations was OSA (Association of Contemporary Architects). Formed in 1925 by Ginsburg and the Vesnin brothers, it also included the LEF group (Leftist Art Front). A. Vesnin became president and Ginsburg vice-president; among the members were Barshch, Burov, Sobolev, Krassilnikov, Vladimirov, Bergman, Gan and many others. In 1926 they started the publication *Contemporary Architecture*; its contributors included Matsa, Pasternak, Nikolsky, Le Corbusier, Leonidov and Sokolov. In 1927 they organized the first architectural exhibition at which countries from abroad were represented. They took part in the International Exhibition in New York.

Members of OSA were exponents of Constructivism and criticized ASNOVA for their antiquated ideas and lack of practical work. OSA was concerned with problems of housing and the new conception of society. They advocated a communal socialist approach to problems within the new economy, and the use of modern techniques. They rejected a purely artistic approach to architecture. Their basic conception of a dwelling was a framework consisting of verticals

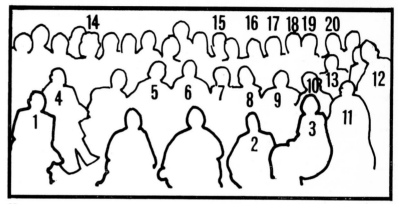

27 First conference of OSA, Moscow 1928.
1 M. Gerchkovich, 2 B. Shtivel,
3 L. Nappelbaum, 4 A. Nikolsky,
5 P. Novitsky, 6 A. Gan, 7 M. Ginsburg,
8 A. Vesnin, 9 V. Vesnin, 10 I. Leonidov,
11 F. Yalovkin, 12 R. Khiger,
13 M. Barshch, 14 T. Chechikova,
15 M. Kholostenko, 16 N. Sokolov,
17 I. Milinis, 18 Kuzmin, 19 G. Orlov,
20 N. Malozemov

27

and horizontals filled with glass surfaces or light partitioning. Competitions were organized. It was essential to reject the pre-Revolutionary methods of building, the degenerate capitalist style, and concentrate on the planning of vital cities and dwellings for the people.

VOPRA

In spite of its many supporters throughout the country, OSA was opposed by VOPRA (the All-Russia Association of Proletarian Architects). Members of VOPRA (Matsa their president, Alabyan, Babenkov, Baburov, Kozelkov, and others) had organized the State Planning Bureau and the Armenian Building Commission, they had worked on the planning of socialist estates such as in Nizhny-Novgorod and were agitating about the development and planning of Moscow. Though aware of the merits of the other societies they accused them of encouraging 'bourgeois art' and utopias. VOPRA refuted eclectic policies which hampered architecture and considered OSA to have gone too far to the left, over-rating the use of technology and rejecting art. Their work was mere imitation of that in the West. To VOPRA architecture had to be proletarian in its form and content – a synthesis of social, economic, emotional, idological and structural elements. It was the application of the dialectics of materialism to planning and experimental work.

In fact the ideas of VOPRA and OSA were very similar; but they were impatient and intolerant and this led to much disagreement and ineffectual discussion.

VANO

In 1929 OSA suggested the creation of a federation of architects in order to co-ordinate their work, reorganize the administration and teaching and improve the standards of building. VANO (Scientific All-Union Association of Architecture) was formed in 1930. It sought the collaboration of ASNOVA, ARU, OSA and VOPRA, and later all those organizations were incorporated – with the exception of VOPRA. The Moscow section became known as MOVANO. VANO campaigned for a single objective – proletarian architecture. The association organized its administration with branches all over the country, K. Dzhus became their first president and soon a five-year plan was evolved. They were to concentrate on theoretical, practical, scientific and technical work in the design of communal housing and a communal socialist structure within industry and agriculture. This involved a synthesis of all their methods together with the study of Marxist–Leninist theory and the sociology of architecture and the fine arts.

SASS

OSA became SASS/VANO and concerned itself with the study of working problems and conditions, industrial settlements, communal housing (the liberation of women and children enslaved in the home), transport and the relationship between city and country. The practical work of SASS (Sector of Architects of Socialist Construction) was not very extensive but they planned the concert hall in Kharkov, the theatre in Sverdlovsk, the Palace of Work in Moscow and similar buildings.

VANO was not confined to professional work and collaborated with other groups such as 'October', 'Izoram', 'Four Arts', 'The Architectural Section of the Painters of the Revolution', and 'Rabis' (architectural section of the Professional Union of Fine Art Workers).

The Party helped considerably towards the establishment of proletarian artists in the fields of fine arts and literature. Nevertheless, the extent of artistic activity was seriously handicapped by the variety of associations and the isolation of many groups, and soon it became evident that a new structure was required. In 1932 all architectural associations were united in the 'Union of Soviet Architects'. Branches were established in all large cities. The first congress of Soviet architects took place in 1937.

(translation Elizabeth Heath)

Unovis

V. Rakitin

UNOVIS was born on the wave of revolution, in the throes of the fight for the reform of art schools and in a turmoil of artistic propaganda; at a time when the first collective attempts were being made to find a new basis for the development of all the arts and the creation of a single popular artistic culture for society.

It was started in the autumn of 1919, when Kazimir Malevich (1879–1935) arrived in Vitebsk from Moscow at the invitation of V. Ermolaeva, Rector of the People's High School of Art and an active adherent of Suprematism. A number of students, who had grouped themselves round Malevich in contradistinction to Marc Chagall and his Talmudic Expressionist group, called themselves 'followers of the new art'. This was contracted to POSNOVIS; a few months later it was changed to UNOVIS, meaning 'founders of the new art'. The letters can also be interpreted as 'affirmation of the new art', when referring to the programme and as 'union of the new art' in relation to society. From the end of 1922 the majority of UNOVIS members worked in Malevich's laboratory in the Petrograd Institute of Artistic Culture, which continued until the end of 1929.

Besides K. Malevich and V. Ermolaeva, the following were members of UNOVIS: I. Chashnik (1902–29), N. Suetin (1897–1954), L. Khidekel, N. Cohen, L. Yudin (1907–41), A. Leporskaya (b. 1904), V. Vorobieva (b. 1900), Nojov, Zeitlin and, until the end of 1921, El Lissitzky (1890–1941) and S. Senkin (b. 1894). G. Klutsis, a well known exponent of Russian Constructivism, was connected with UNOVIS during its early period. The Polish painters Strzminski and Kobro were at the head of the Smolensk branch of UNOVIS, and there were other UNOVIS branches in Petrograd, Moscow, Saratov, Perm, Samara, Odessa and, possibly, in Orenburg and in Minsk. H. Cohen and K. Malevich gave the ideas of UNOVIS wide publicity in the Moscow Museum of Cultural Art in 1922–3.

The theoretical outlook of UNOVIS members in its early (Vitebsk) stage was expressed in some detail in Malevich's book *Of new systems in art*, written in July 1919. This served as a programme and attracted a number of artists. Other writings, *God has been cast off*, *Art*, *The Church* and *The Factory* (1922) were also influential, as were a series of early articles and reports by El Lissitzky in the

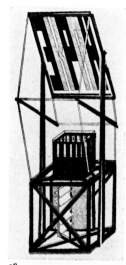

28

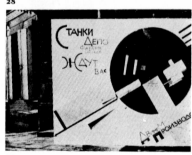

29

28 G. Klutsis: kiosk design, *c.* 1919
29 El Lissitzky: Agit board outside a factory at Vitebsk, 1919

30

31

32

33

30 UNOVIS: tram design, c. 1920
31 Malevich: 'House of the future', 1924
32 N. Suetin: arkhitektoniks, c. 1925
33 UNOVIS group, Vitebsk, 1920 – Malevich is at the blackboard, Suetin on the chair in the foreground

journal *Aero* (published by I. Chashnik and L. Khidekel), together with the UNOVIS wall-newspaper and numerous reports read by the members of UNOVIS at meetings and discussions. K. Malevich summed up the second, Petrograd period, in 'The new generation', a series of articles written for the *Kharkov Journal* during 1928–29, and still praised for their tolerance and breadth of outlook.

Soon after its foundation UNOVIS started publicizing its work abroad: material was sent to Germany in the autumn of 1920 and, a year later, to Kees Beekman in Holland. Lissitzky's articles and the publication of Malevich's book at the Bauhaus also helped to spread the ideas of UNOVIS.

Suprematism, the dominant art philosophy in Russia during the period 1913 to 1917, provided the theoretical basis for the activities

of UNOVIS. The first suprematist experiments in three dimensions
were evolved early in 1914 but developed further only after 1918.
These demonstrate a search for harmony in both the dynamics and
statics of the simplest geometrical forms: forms intersect, producing
a forward thrust of the whole. The basic linear axis, showing the
direction of movement, is accentuated. Geometrical elements are
grouped around it in a single dynamic system. If the planar, two-
dimensional Suprematism – with its fresh colours, reminiscent of
ikons and folk-art – constitutes the ideal industrial ornament, a
starting point for the creation of mural painting, then the problem
of three-dimensional-Suprematism is an architectural one. The
co-ordination of volumes in space logically suggests here not only a
building prototype, but the elaboration of a system for housing
people.

Experiments in the plastic arts led to architectonic solutions and
provided new models for contemporary building. The problem
was to develop building types with particular spaces that were
organically integrated. Architectural expression was to reside in the
particular appropriateness and integrity of each design, in the
ultimate naturalness of its forms – in this not unlike the forms of
nature. There is an unexpected parallel here with some of Frank
Lloyd Wright's ideas. The first architectural models of UNOVIS
members date from 1920. These were called planites,* earthites
and arkhitektoniks. They have complex forms – 'multiformity, a
combination of many elements' – not unlike post-Cubist sculpture.
In later works only the most vital elements remain – necessary not
from the functional point of view, but for the more direct expression
of their plastic form in space. According to many members of
UNOVIS, the essence of architecture lay in such perception. Such an
ideal architecture, it was hoped, would influence world relations
and bring them into harmony. This idea was developed in Malevich's 'theory of the complementary element'. Some forms were
even turned into town plans – N. Suetin's project of 1924, Malevich's of 1927. Members of UNOVIS also worked on designs for
single buildings of a new type – for example the workmen's clubs
of K. Malevich and L. Khidekel. The famous 'Prouns'† of El
Lissitzky must be included among the attempts to find the ideal
architectonic prototype for a new system of plastic art. A feature
common to all members of UNOVIS was the careful attention paid to

* Editor's note: a difficult word to translate while avoiding the English 'planet';
'planit' may be encountered.
† Editor's note: again a compound word. The vowels are pronounced separately:
Pro-un.

34

35

36

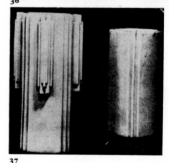

37

34 Malevich: arkhitektoniks, *c.* 1924
35 Malevich: arkhitektoniks, *c.* 1924
36 Cups designed by Malevich, 1923, made
by the Lomonsov factory
37 N. Suetin: vases, 1931

38

39

38 El Lissitzky: title page
from ASNOVA, Moscow, 1926

39 El Lissitzky: final version
of the Lenin podium, 1924

surface finish and to colour, the latter being treated as the bond
between the various elements of the composition. They were also
greatly concerned with the problem of overcoming weight: they
developed the ideas of heliocentrism as a philosophical concept and
in single projects for buildings such as the planite – a kind of
satellite of Earth.

The programme for art education drawn up by UNOVIS was
developed particularly with reference to architecture. Colour,
trends in contemporary art – starting with Cézanne and ending
with Suprematism – were studied first, next various materials and
only then design work. During the Vitebsk period, experimental
work was, to a great extent, combined with poster work and
designs for decorations for revolutionary celebrations. The famous
project for an orator's rostrum was drawn up for such an occasion.
Its author – I. Chashnik – called it the 'rostrum of the sign of
Suprematism'.* It became very popular, in Lissitzky's version, as
the Lenin podium.

* Editor's note: possibly because the base of the rostrum was a red cube. A red
cube was used as a symbol of UNOVIS.

40

41

Prototypes worked out by members of UNOVIS turned out to be truly universal and were successfully applied in various spheres of art. In exhibition design the principle of the dynamic arrangement of spatial components was applied (El Lissitzky, N. Suetin, K. Rozhdestvensky); similarly, in porcelain (N. Suetin, I. Chashnik, A. Leporskaya, K. Malevich), in graphic art (V. Ermolaeva, El Lissitzky, I. Chashnik), and in posters (I. Chashnik, El Lissitzky). They believed that 'all things, the whole world, must be clad in Suprematist forms . . . everything must have Suprematist illustrations, as a new form of harmony'. Experiments were also made in the fields of the theatre and poetry.

In the domain of architecture, there is a lot in common, especially in the manner of working out problems, between UNOVIS and the ASNOVA group, where El Lissitzky immediately felt at home on his return from abroad. In building structures for propaganda and in designing books they worked on parallel lines with the early Constructivists, some of whom (Lyubov Popova, Aleksandr Rodchenko) were active earlier in the field of planar Suprematist painting. However, UNOVIS publicly opposed functional and technical dogma in architecture, though the less rigid of the Constructivist theorists (like Ginsburg) appreciated the contribution of Suprematism to the new type of architecture and rightly compared the work of the members of UNOVIS with the part played in the evolution of contemporary European architecture by adherents of De Stijl. UNOVIS supplied the driving force to Nikolsky's studio in Leningrad and, to some extent, to Leonidov; its influence was also felt in the architecture of the Ukraine of the 1920s.

(translation Marina Corby)

40 Malevich: study for housing in the outskirts of Moscow, 1927

41 Malevich lying in state in his house in Leningrad, 1935

42 I. Chashnik: arkhitektoniks, 1928

Vkhutemas, Vkhutein*

V. Khazanova

43

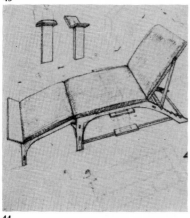

44

The first and second 'Free State Art Studios' were formed in 1918 as a result of a merger between the Moscow School of Painting, Sculpture and Architecture and the Stroganov School. On 29 November 1920, by decree of the RSFSR *Sovnarkom*, the 'Free Studios' were reorganized into the State Higher Art and Technical Studios (VKHUTEMAS). In 1926 a State Higher Art and Technical Institute (VKHUTEIN) was formed as an adjunct to VKHUTEMAS. Apart from the department of general education (preparatory), it included painting, graphics, sculpture, architecture, textile, ceramics, woodwork and metalwork departments.

The faculty of architecture of VKHUTEMAS was formed at the end of 1920. A. Rukhlyadev and I. Rylsky were the deans; the following the principal teachers between 1920 and 1928: N. Baklanov, A. Bakushinsky, N. Buniatov, A. Vesnin, M. Ginsburg, I. Golosov, N. Dokuchaev, A. Efimov, I. Zholtovsky, V. Kokorin, V. Krinsky, A. Kuznetsov, N. Ladovsky, N. Lakhtin, A. Manuilov, K. Melnikov, P. Muratov, E. Norvert, A. Poliakov, K. Ronchevsky, V. Semenov, S. Toropov, S. Chernyshev, D. Shcherbinovsky, A. Shchusev, A. Elkin. The teaching programme for the first and second year courses was based on a psycho-analytical method developed by Ladovsky, professor of the faculty of architecture.

In 1921 the following studios were given equal status with the autonomous 'faculty of architecture' – monumental architecture (Krinsky); planning (Dokuchaev); spatially-decorative architecture (Ladovsky); communal architecture, the 'basic department of discipline instruction' and the experimental model laboratory which was open to all the studios and directed by the architect Efimov.

In November 1922, professors I. Golosov and K. Melnikov organized a new department in the faculty of architecture which they called the 'New Academy' in which they tried to reconcile traditional systems of architectural training with the newest methods of instruction. 'Regulations concerning the faculty of architecture', passed on 3 October 1923, state: 'the faculty is

43 Tubular steel chair designed under the direction of Rodchenko at VKHUTEMAS
44 Chair design by Rodchenko, 1925

* Excerpt from 'History of Soviet Architecture, 1926–1932', issued by the Institute of the History of Art of the Ministry of Culture of the USSR.

45

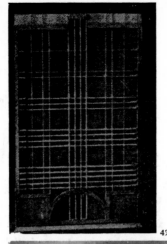

49

46

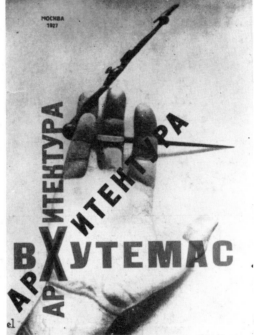

50

47, 48

51

45–8 Successive drawings showing a Constructivist study in the first-year course at VKHUTEMAS

49 Exercise in surface representation (basic course), 1926–27

50 El Lissitzky: cover of the VKHUTEMAS annual, Moscow, 1927

51 VKHUTEIN annual

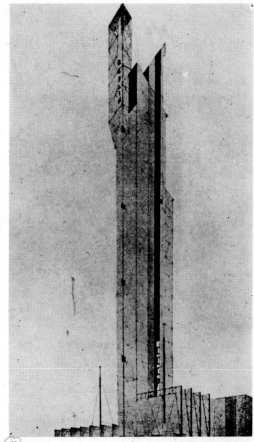

52   53

54   55   56

52 VKHUTEMAS metal workshop, 1925

53 Study in 'control': printing press for *Izvestia*, designed by I. I. Leonidov under the tutorship of A. A. Vesnin, 1926

54 VKHUTEMAS

55 Exercise in the representation of volume (upper part) and space (lower part): water tower, designed by I. V. Lamtsov under the tutorship of N. A. Ladovsky, 1921 (course II)

56 Exercise in representation of mass and weight done under the guidance of V. Krinsky, M. V. Korzhev and S. V. Glagolei (course II)

divided into two ideological groups – the academic, and that searching for new paths in architecture. The two groups are completely autonomous in their approach to problems and in their methods of instruction'. The training in VKHUTEMAS-VKHUTEIN started in the basic department (first- and second-year courses), which provided a general artistic training, and then was taken over

57

by the faculty of architecture proper (third- to fifth-year courses), where the students received a specialized training.

From 1921 onwards Ladovsky consistently demanded a 'research institute', attached to the faculty of architecture for the 'study of the nature of form and its perception'. During 1927–8 he finally managed to organize the architectural laboratory of VKHUTEIN, where scientific research work was carried out under his supervision. In 1928 the architect V. Lavrov wrote: 'The main object of the laboratory is to provide and improve scientific bases for the technical, formal, and sociological sides of architecture, to introduce a new terminology and adapt the existing one to this end'. (*Moscow Building* 1928, No. 10, pp. 14–18.) Ladovsky, as director of the laboratory, constructed a series of devices with the help of which it was possible to test the 'psycho-technical qualities of an architect', and, with the help of the architect A. Krutikov, devised a number of tests (see *Architecture and Vkhutein*, vol. L, Moscow, 1929).

VKHUTEIN was closed in 1930. The Architecture and Building Institute (ASI), soon renamed the Higher Architecture and Building Institute (VASI), was opened in May 1930 for the training of architect-planners and architect-engineers. It was formed from the faculties of architecture of Moscow's Higher Art and Technical Institute (VKHUTEIN-MVKHTI) and the Moscow Higher Technical College. VASI prepared architects for four different specialities: planning, housing, industrial plants and factories and agricultural works.

(translation Marina Corby)

57 Study in 'control': an art school, designed by S. A. Helfeld under the tutorship of N. V. Dokuchaev, 1927

El Lissitzky 1890-1941

V. Rakitin

58 El Lissitzky:
self-portrait, 1924

Eleazar Markovich Lissitzky is one of the few artists of post-Revolutionary Russia whose work is well known in Europe. The rediscovery of Lissitzky in the 1960s was both a recognition of his achievement and an aspect of the search for the sources of Constructivism. Publications and exhibitions since have revealed Lissitzky as not merely a minor abstract painter, but a figure of universal standing. He worked successfully in many different spheres and was endowed with architectural talents. But his various activities are not often related to those of contemporary Europeans; he has appeared to work in a vacuum.[1] When he travelled in Western Europe, at the end of 1921, he was very interested in the latest experiments in art. Yet for his work to be properly understood it must be judged primarily in relation to the atmosphere of the Russian Revolution, with its upheavals and its faith in a radical transformation of the world. In 1917 he completed his architectural degree in Moscow and it is assumed that he was active as an artist from 1912 onwards, initially as an illustrator of books in the manner of Chagall.[2] He himself considered the years he spent in Vitebsk – from summer 1919 to autumn 1921 – as the time of his greatest creative activity. It was then that he reached maturity as architect, typographer and master of exhibition design. It was Chagall who had invited Lissitzky to go to Vitebsk, but Lissitzky knew that Malevich would be teaching there in September 1919 and was eager to further their acquaintance. He had first met him in Moscow the year before, where he had gone in order to see the work of the Suprematists at the 10th State Exhibition of Suprematism and Abstract Art. The exhibition and Malevich himself had both made a great impression on the young architect/designer. In Vitebsk Lissitzky taught at the Studio of Graphic Arts, Printing and Architecture at the People's High School of Art. He wanted students to be able to learn 'the basic methods and systems of architecture and to develop the graphic and plastic expression of their constructional projects through the use of *models*'.[3] It was in connection with such models that the 'Proun' projects were first initiated in autumn 1919. They were a logical

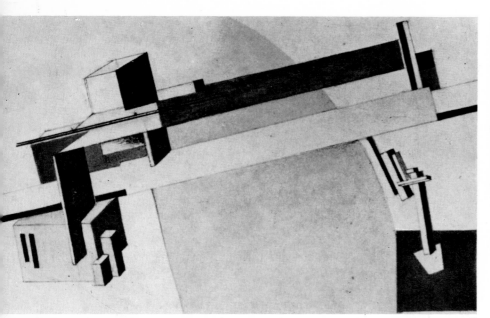

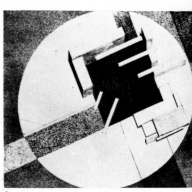

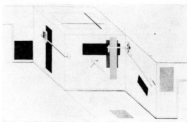

59

60

61

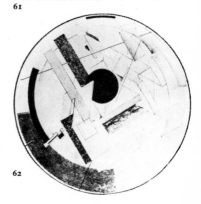

62

outcome of his study of Suprematism. Comparison with Malevich's work makes this obvious.

The 'Prouns' were developed in collaboration with other pupils of Malevich – who in 1921 succeeded Chagall as principal of the Vitebsk school. 'Prouns' were shown first at an exhibition in Vitebsk in 1919 as paintings, though Lissitzky himself regarded 'Prouns', as well as similar designs by other followers of Malevich, as a transitional stage between painting and architecture. He used them as a means of studying the relationship between form and material, colour and material, material and construction. Leaving the painting and the artist on one side and the machine and engineer on the other, the 'Proun' proceeds to create a new space.[4] The 'Proun' is the structural element in a new system of spatial composition – the basis of which was Malevich's 'black square'. With it Lissitzky demonstrated the depth of space and emphasized the mass of form, yet it is wrong to consider the 'Proun' as a spatial element just as it is wrong to think of contemporary Suprematist projects by other members of UNOVIS – the 'founders of the new art' – as planar.[5] For Suprematism was developing at Vitebsk as an art of form-making – of architecture. The 'Proun' did not emerge in isolation, but as a part of the assimilation of the lessons of

59 El Lissitzky: Proun IA, bridge I, 1919
60 El Lissitzky: Proun IE, the town, 1921
61 El Lissitzky: Proun room, Berlin Art Exhibition, 1923
62 El Lissitzky: Proun 6B, 1921

Suprematism. It reflects the explanatory efforts of the art of the period. There are, however, obvious differences between 'Prouns' and the models made by Lissitzky's colleagues. His models are more dynamic and decisively orientated in space and, though it may seem paradoxical, the abstraction of the 'Proun' often conceals a concrete architectural intention.

'Prouns' contain different spatial constructions that often have definite connotations – as in Bridge 'Proun' 1 A, 1919; or Town 'Proun' I-E, 1921 (shown at the Exhibition of Russian Art in Berlin in 1922). This last is close to the architectural models of Malevich, Chashnik and Suetin. 'Proun' 30 E is in essence a scenic design. Many of the problems postulated in the 'Prouns' – overcoming weight, the free soaring of forms – have found solutions in such projects as that for a horizontal skyscraper in Moscow [the so-called 'Cloudprop' project]. 'Prouns' have also formed the basis of practical design. As a member of the Central Creative Committee of UNOVIS, Lissitzky was directly involved in propaganda.[6] In his town-planning propaganda panels and posters, he emphasized the dynamic essence of the impact of colour forms in Suprematist space. For him they symbolized social issues – as in the intrusion of an intensely red triangle into a pure white circle in the poster 'Beat the Whites with the Red Wedge' (1920).

Propaganda required single-minded perception. The conjunction of spatial experiments with 'Prouns' and Malevich's ideas on the display of museum exhibits,[7] soon led to the elaboration of new principles for setting up exhibitions. A complex and heterogeneous mass of exhibits became, in Lissitzky's hands, a well ordered whole. His exhibits were worked out like a film; the best directly relating to the Cologne Exhibition of 1928, and to the film montage methods of Dziga Vertov. Lissitzky met Vertov through Malevich and Eisenstein in 1925. The display was arranged in such a way that the viewer could not miss the most important exhibits. His route was planned like the movements of an actor on the stage. A particular object of the display was that the viewer should not absorb it passively, he should be involved in the show. In this way, Lissitzky realized in exhibition art the spatial concepts of post-Cézanne painting, where the viewer feels that he is not only the standard, the module, but, to some extent, the centre of the composition. It is clear that in exhibition art – and Lissitzky considered that his prime activity – he synthesized other traditions. He was impressed by the Soviet pavilion designed by K. Melnikov for the Paris International Exhibition of 1925; it was, however, rather his

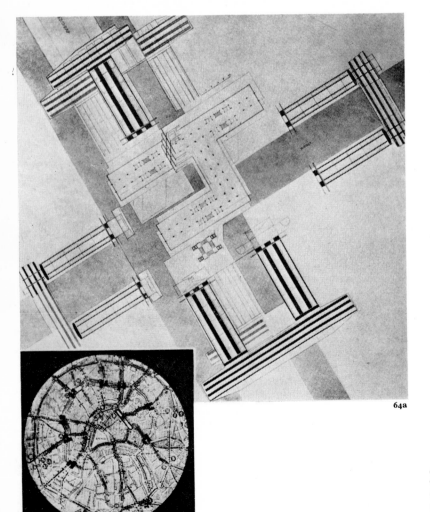

63 El Lissitzky: Cloudprops (*Wolkenbugel*)
on Nikitsky Square, Moscow, 1925

64a El Lissitzky: Cloudprop, 1924

64b El Lissitzky: Moscow city centre with
Cloudprops around the inner ring road

65

66

own experiments, particularly during the period of propaganda work in Vitebsk,[8] that formed the basis of his developed style – though naturally this changed with time. It became sharper, more dynamic, closer to Constructivism. This is evident in his successive alterations to the design for the Lenin podium in 1924 (the first project was by I. Chashnik, 1920). He increased the forward thrust of the podium, sharpened the angle of inclination over the square and revealed more clearly the intricacies of the structure itself, giving to the podium a greater emotional impact.

During the Vitebsk period Lissitzky was already trying to integrate various techniques in one art form. Typical of such experiments were the designs for the futurist poet Kruchenykh's electromechanical puppet play *Victory over the Sun* (music by M. Matiushin). This was designed in competition with V. Ermolova, who based her programme on abstract painting (this was staged early in 1921); Lissitzky, however, demonstrated the full aesthetic possibilities of future theatrical techniques.

The conjunction of 'Prouns' and propaganda design led to new methods of book production. Typography assumed a new vitality, though in fact Lissitzky's general approach resembled that already adopted in other spheres; for instance, the composition of *The Red has stopped* may be compared to that of the *Tale of Two Squares* (1920) – a red square, it should also be noted, was stitched on the sleeves of the jackets and coats of all UNOVIS members. And all have something in common with the design for the horizontal skyscraper of 1923 to 1925. The similarity lies not only in the outward form, the repetition of the basic formal elements, but in the attitudes first adopted. Later, in 1931, Lissitzky himself expressed this in the following formula: 'For whom + for what purpose + what = how'.[9]

At this point Lissitzky departed for Western Europe. He absorbed omnivorously all that appealed to him in the European art of the 1920s. In turn he publicized the ideas evolved in Russia during the revolutionary years. He was one of the few men of the period able to reconcile such divergent sources of inspiration. The 'binding element', in his case, was an acceptance of artistic expediency in the light of the firm conviction that art had a social function.

He was guided in all things by this principle. He did not repeat the experiments of the Vitebsk period, but instead constantly changed both his forms and techniques. He made wide use of photo-montage in book illustration, which he considered a most

65 El Lissitzky: poster for Russian exhibition, Zurich, 1929

66 El Lissitzky with his model for the Meyerhold theatre, 1929

67

67 Meeting in Dusseldorf, 1922, left to right, Werner Graeff, Raoul Hausmann, Theo van Doesburg, Carel van Eesteren, Hans Richter, Nelly van Doesburg, unidentified, El Lissitzky, Ruggero Vasari, Hannah Hoch, Kurt Seiwert

effective and expressive way of mass communication.[10] The elegant abstraction of the 'Prouns' was replaced in the Zurich Exhibition of 1930 by the hypnotic, almost surrealist effects of his posters. It is interesting to note that one of them served as model for Mucha's statue *The Workman and the Member of the Kolkhoz* – the emblem of the Soviet pavilion at the Paris Exhibition of 1937.

Lissitzky also turned to the study of furniture and standardized units. In order to achieve harmony in design, he held it was necessary to delve deeply into the fundamentals of style. And he posed the following basic principles for forms (these were not meant to apply to furniture alone):

(a) expressiveness and tectonic structure
(b) expressiveness of volume, combination of volumes, and space formation
(c) standard requirements
(d) proportions and module
(e) rhythm in furniture. . . .[11]

Few artists have been as receptive to current ideas as Lissitzky; equally, few men have been as true to their time and have so firmly believed in the inexhaustible possibilities of progress or in the re-shaping of the whole of man's material and spatial environment.

(translation Marina Corby)

1 Exceptions to such interpretations are the recent publications: *El Lissitzky* VEB Verlag Kunst 1967, the catalogue of the exhibition *Avantgarde Osteuropa* 1910–30, Berlin 1967, and the extremely interesting book by Troels Anderson *Moderñe russisk Kuñst 1910–1925*, Copenhagen 1967.

2 Concerning Lissitzky's Jewish illustrations see the article in the *Studio* October 1966, p. 182. Other influences may have included M. Dobuzhinsky's work for the World of Art periodical (*Mir Iskusstva*) and handwritten Futurist volumes.

3 *Journal of the Government Soviet of Peasant, Red Army Worker and Labourer Deputies*, 1919, No. 169 of 17 July, p. 3.

4 Quoted from the Russian text of the article, 'Not a world vision, but a world reality', UNOVIS 1920 – TSGALI, f. 2361, ed. store 25, p.14, better known under the name 'Proun'. This article appeared in *De Stijl* 1922, no. 6, reprinted in the Dresden edition of 1967.

5 Many others are of this opinion, among them D. Khelm, author of one of the best of the recent articles on Lissitzky: *Avantgarde Osteuropa* 1910–1930, Berlin 1967, pp. 28–32.

6 Lissitzky took an active part in the Vitebsk 'Windows of Growth' and collaborated with the Political Government of the Central Front. In 1920 he represented UNOVIS at the All-Russia Propaganda Congress in Orenburg, as instructor.

7 During those years Malevich was engaged in planning a radical re-organization of museums and of exhibition design in general.

8 Other members of UNOVIS – I. Chashnik, K. Rozhdestvensky, and, especially, N. Suetin – became masters of exhibition design at this time.

9 Unpublished report in the Moscow House of Printing about designing books. Quoted from an article by S. Telingater, 'The New Art of Design in the USSR', in the journal *Artists' Brigade*, Moscow 1931, No. 4, p. 23.

10 The first experiments in photo-montage in Soviet Russia were made in 1919 (A. Khan, G. Klutsis).

11 Unpublished report 'Artistic reasons for the standardization of individual civilian furniture', 1928 – TSGALI, f. 2361, ed. store 30, p. 18.

The Vesnin Brothers

A. Chinyakov

'It fell to us to forge the language of the new architecture when we had to cut down on every cubic metre of the construction, every barrel of cement and every kilo of nails.'

When the October Revolution occurred the three Vesnin brothers were already established as practising architects. They had begun to enter architectural competitions together at the beginning of the war, Leonid contributing a solid academic background, Viktor an incisive and analytical mind and Aleksandr a great artistic talent, to form a unified and harmonic whole.

Their first major independent work was a house built for D. V. Sirotkin in 1914–15 at Nizhny-Novgorod. Their client posed them various problems. Not only was the style to be classical, as Sirotkin wished to donate the house to the city as a museum upon his death, but in addition to this, Sirotkin demanded premises that complied with traditional Russian customs. The brothers succeeded in giving the building the attributes of Russian classicism, avoiding unnecessary stylization: the interiors were laid out simply and with taste, and the ceiling of the great hall was decorated with paintings by Aleksandr. The building, however, did not entirely emerge from its pre-Revolutionary context of insipid eclecticism, where styling was borrowed from Russian Classicism, Italian Renaissance and traditional Russian architecture. However, it is interesting to note that in an early variant of the project continuous fenestration was planned for the whole height of the corner rooms on the first floor. This would have given the building a more contemporary appearance but the idea was later dropped, perhaps because it was in obvious discord with the classical details of the façade.

Other projects, including designs for a theatre at Yaroslavl (1908) and for the racing stables and jockey club at the Moscow Hippodrome (1914), testify to a broader eclecticism and reveal the architects ringing the changes on various styles.

Industrial architecture, long considered unworthy of the architect's attention, was to help V. A. Vesnin, and his brothers after him, to escape the stifling atmosphere of eclecticism. A new field of activity was opened up that permitted new statements, in

68

69

70

68 Viktor A. Vesnin
69 Leonid A. Vesnin
70 Aleksandr A. Vesnin

which the history of styles played no part whatsoever. Its demands upon the architect were instead knowledge of the production process, functional planning, and logical economical techniques of construction.

The influence that working on industrial buildings exerted on the work of the Vesnin brothers can first be seen in their last major work before the Revolution – designs for the universal store of the Dinamo joint stock company, to be erected in Lubyansky Square, Moscow. The Vesnin brothers received the commission after entries submitted by other architects had been rejected. Their designs struck a blow in favour of clarity in architectural composition, relinquishing all elements of stylization.

The reinforced-concrete frame of the five-storey building allowed the architects to eliminate structural walls and to envisage each floor as one large well-lit trading area. Whereas external decorations had once concealed the structure of earlier designs and buildings, they now became an integral element of the whole architectural composition. The simple rectangular volume of the building, rhythmically divided up by a well-proportioned translucent arcade appropriate to the vertical rhythm of the frame, together with the scarcity of decorative details, all helped to create a new and fresh appearance for the store, variations of which have been erected up to this day.

The Dinamo project serves as a connecting link between the work produced by the Vesnin brothers before and after the Revolution. The various features of the new architecture which it illustrates found their logical fulfilment a few years later in the project of the Palace of Labour, the Arcos building and the building for the newspaper *Leningrad Pravda*.

The Revolution did not hinder the brothers' creative partnership. Unlike some of their colleagues they did not find it difficult to adopt new attitudes towards architecture. They later wrote in a declaration of their creative principles: 'It was clear to us that we could no longer work in our former manner. A new era in the history of mankind had begun. The storms and waves of the Revolution swept away everything that impeded the development of the new life. Architects were faced with the problem of keeping in step with the builders of the new life, of assisting in the work of consolidating the position achieved, and of discerning the new problems that life presented.' Far from remaining words on paper, this commitment was fulfilled in the brothers' practical work.

We should note at this point that such a committed, unequivocal

71

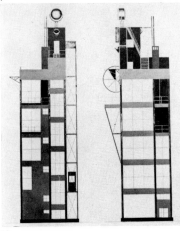

72

71 Vesnin brothers: project for Arcos store, 1924

72 A. A. and V. A. Vesnin: project for the *Leningrad Pravda* building, Moscow, 1924

position at that time led to a situation that was not always easy.
For his part in the first May Day celebrations in Red Square in
1918 Viktor Vesnin was immediately dismissed from the designers'
office in which he was then working.

The almost total cessation of building in the first years after the
Revolution did not leave the Vesnin brothers inactive. On the
invitation of the sculptor S. Aleshin they took part, in 1919, in
a competition for a projected monument to Karl Marx in Moscow.
In this project no attempt was made to create the usual sort of a
portrait monument, but rather to express the very idea of Marxism.
Viktor Vesnin outlined the basic idea of the monument as follows:
'The monument to Marx is not simply a monument to a specific
person; it is also a monument to a great historical idea under whose
star passes the whole of the present-day evolution of man'.

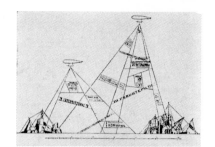

73

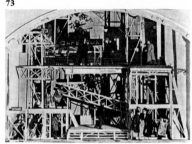

74

The monument represented a dynamic group with Marx at its
head, as the leader of the world's proletariat, symbolizing the
leading role of the party and its indissoluble ties with the working
class. Lenin favoured the project. The foundations of the
monument were solemnly laid in spring 1920 and Vladimir Ilych
Lenin delivered a speech. However, the temporary model of the
monument suffered the same fate as other temporary monuments
erected in accordance with Lenin's plan for a monumental propaganda.

Aleksandr Vesnin's talent as a theatrical designer was to shine
brilliantly in those years of restricted architectural activity. In
1919–20 he staged several productions at the Maly Theatre.
However, after the theatre refused to use his sets for A. V.
Lunacharsky's play *Oliver Cromwell* because they were too 'leftist'
(though Lunacharsky himself praised one of the stage-sets by 'the
extraordinarily talented Vesnin') Aleksandr left the Maly Theatre,
and in the summer of 1920 worked with Vsevolod Meyerhold on
celebrations for the Third Congress of the Communist International. Subsequently he turned his great talent to the Kamerny
Theatre where together with the producer A. Ya. Tairov he executed
a series of brilliant sets that included designs for Racine's *Phèdre*
(1922) and Chesterton's *The Man who was Thursday* (1923).

When considering the theatrical works of Aleksandr Vesnin it
is essential to realize the fact that the artist of *Phèdre* and *The Man
who was Thursday* is using the same language as the architects of the
Palace of Labour and *Leningrad Pravda* projects. Linked together
they represent that unified creative tendency that came to be called
'Constructivism'. The meaning of the term 'Constructivism' in

73 L. Popova and A. Vesnin: Design for a
mass festival organized by Meyerhold, 1920
74 A. Shchusev and V. Vesnin: Set for
G. K. Chesterton's *The Man who was
Thursday*, as it appeared when presented at
Kamerny Theatre, Moscow, 1923

Soviet architecture remains unclear and ill-defined to this day, because the architects working under the flag of 'Constructivism' expressed very varied and often diametrically opposed viewpoints in matters of principle, and for many 'Constructivism' was simply a fashionable development in the architecture of the 1920s. It is important therefore to underline that the Vesnin brothers always occupied an independent position within this movement, consistent in its principles and, in many cases, distinct even from the positions of their colleagues in the Union of Contemporary Architects (OSA) which was formed with their active participation in 1925. They did not deny the importance of those aspects of architecture concerned with aesthetics or with formal content or of the necessity of remaining critically aware of their architectural inheritance. Nor did they share the abstract dogmatism of certain other theoreticians of Constructivism on other matters.

We have seen that in their creative declaration the Vesnin brothers had maintained that Soviet architecture was called upon to 'discern the new problems set by life'. In connection with this it became evident to them that it was necessary to create a new architecture relevant to the new Constructive epoch, and that the road they sought lay in the reflection and organization of the new living processes.

'We are convinced that the new forms of Soviet architecture will be found not by way of the imitation of the architectural forms of the past, but on a basis of critical thinking, as in the past, so now, by way of a profound understanding of living processes and their translation into architectural form.'

Speaking from long personal experience of working with the Vesnins, I can affirm that by 'Constructivism' they certainly did not understand abstract dogma or an architectural style, but rather a whole system of architectural thought. When working on an expedient and functional resolution of a plan in accordance with specifications, the architect at once decides the spatio-volumetric organization of the building while striving for an organic unity of form and content. In their opinion this is the architect's main problem. Particularly in the Vesnins' earliest works after the Revolution there is a seeking for new architectural forms that will respond more fully to the demands of Soviet man's new way of life. Their basis for this lay in the use of new materials and the investigation of their new constructive and artistic possibilities.

In those years when actual building was only put in train when

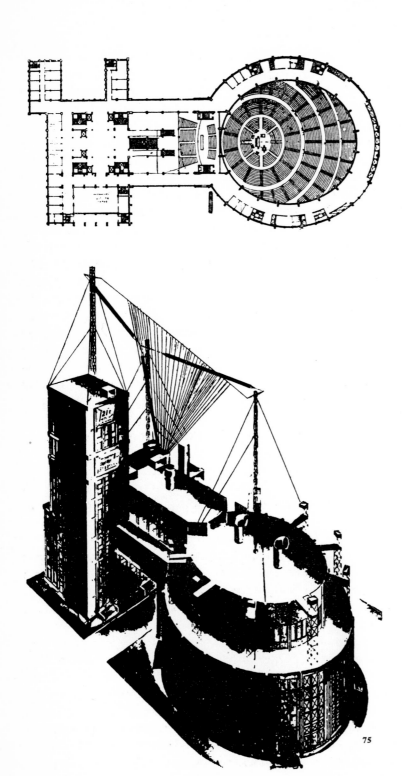

75

75, 76 A. A. and L. A. Vesnin: Palace of Work 1922–23

76

absolutely necessary, what accounted for much of the development of architects' creative thought were the architectural competitions for designs for new types of building called into existence by the Revolution – workers' clubs and flats, and the houses of the communes.

The competition of 1922 for an enormous Palace of Labour in Moscow was the first large-scale architectural competition to follow the Revolution. The Vesnin brothers submitted designs to the competition jury at the beginning of 1923. These were outstanding in their approach to Palace architecture, previously always associated with pomp and richness of architectural forms. Instead of fulfilling the competition requirements which demanded a stone building of 'rich and palatial appearance', the Vesnin brothers presented designs for a ferro-concrete building totally lacking in 'rich' decorative ornament, contrasting sharply in its strength and simplicity with the pompous, palatial residences of the past. Concrete expression is found of Aleksandr Vesnin's dictum that 'architecture should not seek assistance from the other arts, it must be beautiful and expressive in itself'. At the same time one cannot deny that the ascetic severity of the architectural language appears excessively plain and over-simplified. Doubtless this is indicative not only of the 'severe spirit of the time', but also of a sharp reaction away from the unrestrained eclecticism of pre-Revolutionary architecture.

A most remarkable aspect of the design was its exceptionally complete resolution of an enormous building containing rooms for the most diverse purposes. These included a large auditorium with 8000 seats, a hall for meetings of the Mossoviet (the Moscow Committee of the Party), with seating for 2500, auditoria for lectures (seating for 1000 and 500 people), a library, reading rooms, a social museum, a dining room (capacity 1500), other rooms for the Mossoviet, and finally, a powerful central radio station. A huge hall of oval plan, 75 by 67 metres in diameter, was envisaged, having something of the appearance of an ancient amphitheatre but without the traditional tiers, balconies and rows to divide up the public. By means of a movable wall the two main halls could be united to raise the seating capacity to 10,500. Administrative and other official rooms were centred in the top half of the building. The radio station, which was the crowning feature of the building and which presented a network of antennae that recurred as a feature of several new projects, stood as a world-wide tribute to the victorious proletariat.

The competition jury included representatives of the old academic
school who were unhappy about the extraordinary appearance of
the project. A. V. Shchusev, the academician and their president,
subsequently recalled that they had concluded that it was not
possible to give the first prize to this project as 'the architecture was
on the wrong track'. The Vesnins' project received only third
prize. 'Nevertheless,' said Shchusev, 'architecture developed in the
new direction.' The new direction was far from evident, however,
and the search for it provoked many quarrels and disagreements
between various architectural unions and groups.

Shchusev once jokingly commented in conversation with
Viktor Vesnin that 'Nowadays whichever architects you turn to,
whether you go to OSA, ARU or ASNOVA you find new trends. Everything
used to be much simpler and clearer. The gentry or aristocracy
went to Fomin for designs, merchants to Zholtovsky and brothers
of the church turned to me. We each knew our own diocese and we
never quarrelled or squabbled.' This remark, of course, contained
an element of truth: architectural clients before the Revolution
belonged essentially to these social categories, and each had its own
'favourite' architect. The Revolution completely changed this
situation and a new collective client, the government of the workers
and peasants, the workers' organizations, emerged to replace the old
estates. New demands in architecture were the natural consequence.

In the designs submitted for the Palace of Labour competition
the Vesnin brothers, in their own words, had 'set themselves the
aim of creating the architectural form of a new palace – the palace
of the nation's masses. Along with this, we considered that the only
way to discover this form was through a properly architectural
organization of the plan, and through the translation of social and
utilitarian functions into the terms of an architecture that expresses
the content of the building. While working on the plan, we simultaneously studied the sections, façades, perspectives, axonometrics;
in a word, the entire volumetric and spatial composition in full.
This inevitably produced the concrete form of the palace of the
masses.'

It is obvious from this explanation that the Vesnins did not adopt
a negative attitude to the importance of the aesthetic and formal
qualities of architecture, though their position in relation to this
question remained ill-defined.

A very careful answer once given by Viktor Vesnin to A. V.
Lunacharsky attests to this; asked directly if he considered work on
architectural form significant in any way he replied:

'I belong to that tendency and group which does not consider it essential to separate a building into elements of architecture as distinct from elements of engineering. The form in a given circumstance emerges only as a result. If we do work on the form, then it is only to render more precise and perfect its expression of those given facts. This gives one a basic functional solution. I can only answer you in this way.'

However, all their statements about the manner in which architectural form is derived from the demands of the building in no way prevented the Vesnins from lending it their most serious attention when engaged in practical design work.

Perhaps the best way to sense what is characteristic about the Vesnins' 'Constructivism' is to compare two roughly contemporary competition entries: the Vesnins' Palace of Labour project and the *Chicago Tribune* project by Walter Gropius.

At first glance both projects appear to have something in common but on closer inspection this turns out to be nothing more than the logical method of expressing the frame construction of the building on its exterior; their similarity begins and ends here. The spatial composition of the *Chicago Tribune* scarcely deviates from the normal type of American tall building. Gropius merely liberates his façade from external decorative encumbrances, completely opening up the whole screen of the ferro-concrete frame which is marked in only a few places by horizontal balconies to enliven the tedious monotony of the units within the frame's network. Inside is the normal standard office building

In the Palace of Labour project the monolithic and total volumetric-spatial composition of the building forms an organic whole that grows logically from its complex plan. No modification is possible without disrupting the overall architectural form of the building. The ferro-concrete framework is emphatically revealed on the exterior, though this is not evident at all points. It does not simply have the appearance of a neutral or mechanical network of verticals and horizontals as it is precisely calculated to emphasize the monumentality of the building, and, simultaneously, to bind together all the various components of the architectural composition into a unified whole.

In this example one sees how the Vesnins' Constructivism developed along its own lines from the first, and was distinct in principle from Western European Constructivism. Their work contrasted with the latter in which architecture was almost inevitably subordinated to purely functional and technical demands. The basis of the Vesnins' creative method was the essential social aspect of architecture. Painstaking work on the functional expediency of a plan, and a determination to remain abreast of modern building techniques, never overshadowed in their works the important and new social content of Soviet architecture which helped them to define the most accurate solutions to the new public building problems.

77 Vesnin brothers: plan and elevation of Mostorg Store, 1926

The Palace of Labour project marked the beginning of a new stage in the Vesnins' development. It was also the concrete expression of the principles of a new architecture, responding, through the conviction of its authors, to the new demands of the Soviet people and to their new world outlook. It was their first endeavour to create a building that was new both in its social type and also in the artistic expression of the ideas it contained. Despite the fact that the Palace of Labour was never executed, one cannot simply assign it to a category of 'paper' projects, for its influence upon the wide-ranging developments in Soviet and foreign architecture was without doubt of more consequence than that of many other executed buildings. Later works by the Vesnin brothers continued with varying degrees of success to develop the same principles most precisely and distinctly expressed in the Palace of Labour project. Among them one must count the projected Arcos building, the Moscow offices of the newspaper *Leningrad Pravda* (1924), the store on Krasnaya Presna (1927), and workers' clubs in Moscow, Ivanov and Baku (1926–8) as well as competition designs for the Lenin library (1928) and other buildings.

The end of the 1920s and the early 1930s constituted the culminating period of the Vesnin brothers' work – to it belong those three projects which most completely and in all respects characterize their principles: work on the Dneproges dam and power station (1929), the project for an enormous theatre at Kharkov (1930) and the ZIL Palace of Culture in Moscow (1931).

The architectural competition for the then largest hydro-electric power station in Europe (on the river Dneiper) graphically demonstrated both the merits and de-merits of having architects to design industrial buildings. In the designs presented by members of the 'academic school', that is I. V. Zholtovsky and V. A. Shchuko, and in designs presented by American consultants who had worked on the *Dneprostroy* (Dneiper dam), two diametrically opposed concepts of industrial architecture emerged. The American project worked out the technical aspects of this engineering structure while

78–81 Vesnin brothers: project for the Lenin Library, Moscow, 1928

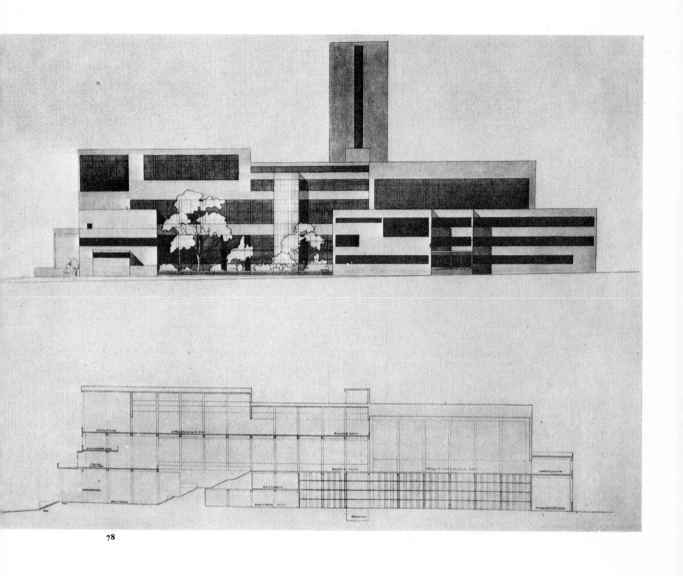

78

79

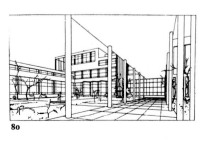

80

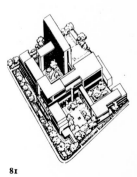

81

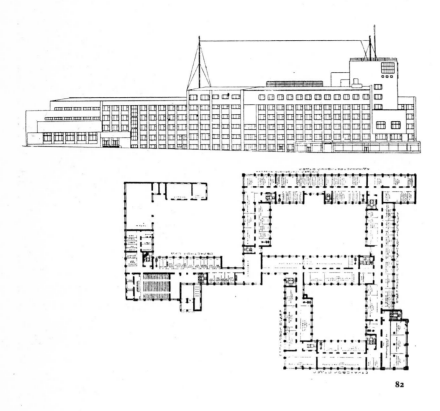

82

82 V. A. and A. A. Vesnin: project for
executive committee of Sverdlovsk, 1926

totally neglecting the aesthetic demands of its architecture; in the
other projects the engineering fabric, sometimes even to the
detriment of the internal technological process, was diligently
covered in rich architectural decoration with great mastery in an
Italian Renaissance or more up-to-date 'modern' style.

It was finally decided that the project should be carried out
under the direction of Viktor Vesnin by a group of architects
(N. Ya. Kolli, G. M. Orlov and S. G. Andriyevsky), and he
successfully united the utilitarian and engineering requirements
of the building with architecture of the highest aesthetic quality.
The hydro-electric power station was only a part of an involved
building complex. The smooth curve of the dam, measured in an
even rhythm by its concrete abutments, tied into a whole the
electro-power station flanking it on one side, and the floodgates on
the other side. The enormous scale and clear, simple architectural
volumes devoid of petty details together constitute an imposing

83

83 V. Vesnin, N. Kolli, G. Orlov,
S. Andriyevsky, V. Corchinsky: the
Dneiper dam

architectural ensemble, a symbol of man's struggle with the
natural elements, and his victory over them.

In the words of A. V. Lunacharsky, one of the judges of the
competition designs: 'Vesnin has brought together power, lightness
and fitness in the architecture of an industrial building.' He
especially pointed out in his comments that 'There is an enormous
gulf between American and Soviet industrialization. It rises out of
the fact that our working class is not in the service of industry, but
industry is in the service of the working class, and that the workers'
settlement is not merely an appendage of the factory but the factory

84

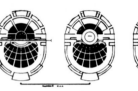

85

forms the basis of the health and well-being of the settlement. The important problem is the construction of a healthy, human way of life, that existence worthy of man in which Marx saw the final aim of socialism, this is what we must be aware of.'

A practical affirmation of this thought was the well-planned, modern and well-organized town of Bolshoi Zaporozhe, built contemporaneously with the Dneproges power station and among the first examples of Soviet city building.

The international competition for a 'theatre of man's musical activities' at Kharkov, then the capital of the Ukraine, attracted a great number of participants. 144 projects were presented for this new type of theatre. The requirements of the competition were that the stage and auditorium should constitute a unified whole, as they were intended not only for the usual theatrical events but also for mass activities popular at that time, national festivals, demonstrations, meetings, sporting activities, circuses and the theatrical treatment of important themes calling for the active participation of the spectators.

The Vesnins envisaged a huge single auditorium, as in their project for the Palace of Labour. A specially devised constructional arrangement of the stage made it possible to change its dimensions easily and simultaneously to alter the capacity of the auditorium from 2000 to 6000 seats. The round auditorium formed the core of the plan and of the external volume of the building; it was built like an amphitheatre but covered by a sloping cupola. Outside, the hall was half surrounded by the foyer and the halls adjacent to the 'stage box'. In this project the most complex acoustic problems were brilliantly resolved. Wide use was made of new developments

84, 85 L. A., A. A. and V. A. Vesnin: plans and sketch of the state theatre, Kharkov, 1931, showing transformations of the stage area in theatrical technology. The customary flights of stairs were replaced by a system of slopes that permitted the hall to be occupied and vacated with ease and comfort.

The competition jury allocated the first prize to the Vesnin brothers, considering their work 'by far the best of all the projects in the competition'. However, the project finally remained un-realized after the transfer of the capital of the Ukraine from Kharkov to Kiev.

'We consider one of our most successful works,' wrote the Vesnins, 'to have been the competition designs for the theatre at Kharkov. To a degree we had achieved an organic architectural whole that united interior with exterior organization, and details with the overall design. There was also clarity and legibility in the construction of the volumes, in the creation of the forum of the new mass theatre. The Dneiper hydro-electric power station we also count amongst our best works. In that project the architecture was organically bound up with the station's workings, with the dam and with the natural landscape in the vicinity.'

With the growth of industrialization and the expansion of socialist building, the need for workers' clubs was superseded by a demand for much larger 'Palaces of Culture' serving as centres for whole urban areas. One such Palace of Culture was planned by the Union of Metalworkers in the proletarian region of the capital. Workers in the factories there (Amo, Dinamo and other large concerns) took a most active part in discussing the preliminary questions and in later discussions of the competition projects. The workers held meetings to criticize the inadequacies of individual projects and to introduce their own specific wishes. At times the hall of the club of the Dinamo factory could not hold all those wishing to take part in the discussion of the projects. Thus the Vesnins' designs, which were eventually accepted, arose as a result of a friendly co-operation between the architects and their collective client – workers of the proletarian region who had contributed days of unpaid labour, long before the final approval of the designs, clearing the ground for construction of the future Palace of Culture on the site of the former Simonov monastery. They worked under the slogan 'Let us build the home of our culture on the site of the home of obscurity'.

The architectural complex which constituted the new Palace of Culture was to include a theatre and other unexecuted build-ings, as well as various club amenities. By 1931–4 only the club itself had been completed. It included a small hall for gatherings and cinema, a library, reading rooms for children and adults, scientific and technical workshops, exhibition rooms, a restaurant, a winter garden, lecture rooms, and an astronomical observatory with a revolving dome situated on the flat roof.

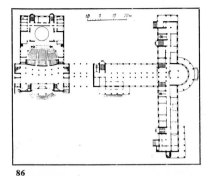

86

The compact architectural composition of the body of the club co-ordinated the various constituent elements into an organic whole. The Vesnin brothers worked out with characteristic diligence an internal scheme that allowed for separate rooms that interconnected, as well as more isolated 'quiet' or 'noisy' rooms for adults or children and so on. The architecture of the building is characteristically modest and simple and every effort is made to create a sensation of freedom and spaciousness within what the Vesnin brothers designated 'interflowing' space.

Close attention was paid to economic questions and the Vesnin brothers were proud that the cost per cubic metre of the building was unprecedentedly low. The erected part of the complex – the club – is now known as the ZIL Palace of Culture. Though substantially ruined by recent alterations and insensitive redecoration of the interiors (dating from the period of lavish architectural embellishment), nevertheless, it can still stand as an example of a well considered plan with an admirably simple outward form.

87

The death of Leonid A. Vesnin in October 1933 caused the creative partnership to lose its oldest comrade. This coincided with a growing tendency in Soviet architecture towards the elaboration and embellishment of architecture, a passion for luxurious external decoration totally at odds with the creative methods of the Vesnin brothers. However, they showed great courage in remaining solitary champions of expediency, truthfulness and simplicity in architecture, refusing to become involved in the general stream of fashion or to sacrifice their principles to a prevalent taste.

(translation John Milner)

88

[This article has been adapted from the Russian essay 'Brat'ya Vesniny' by A. Chinyakov in *Arkhitektura SSSR* No. 3, 1967, pp. 41–54. For reasons of space a discussion of the early years of the Vesnin brothers has been deleted – EDITOR]

86–88 A. A. & L. A. Vesnin: ZIL Palace of Culture, Vostochnaya Ulitsa, Moscow, 1933 (competition 1930). Photos: Urs Graf

Konstantin Melnikov

Yu. Gerchuk

The seventy-fifth birthday of Konstantin Stepanovich Melnikov, one of the founders of Soviet architecture, was celebrated by Moscow architects with an evening in his honour and a large exhibition of his work.

In the history of the architecture of the 1920s and early 1930s, Melnikov has become well known for his creative work, which perhaps shows the brilliance and almost grotesque refinement of expression of one deeply involved in the conflicting architectural tendencies of his day. He has been exalted and he has been deni- grated and the reverberations of these arguments resound to this day. However, for the main part the animosity occasioned by the name of Melnikov is founded upon misunderstandings and prejudices strengthened by the passage of time, although their basis has long disappeared.

Today it is possible to review Melnikov's creative development objectively. The logic of this material will oblige critics to recognize the partial and personal nature of their attitudes. I myself cannot claim in this essay to present an impartial assessment or detailed review of the merits and deficiencies of all the products or even of all the periods of Melnikov's work. This essay is rather an attempt to describe the particular character of his architectural thought.

Melnikov completed his studies at the Moscow College of Painting, Sculpture and Architecture in 1917. Like everyone else he produced, as part of his studies, projects for halls in the Roman style, Neoclassical railway stations, and churches in the Russian style. The student Melnikov of 1916 and the young architect Melnikov at the beginning of the 1920s had very little in common.

Melnikov was among the first architects to seek new forms in response to the demands of new undertakings. The 1920s favoured fantasy. The Revolution, which had opened up new areas of thought, gave an extraordinarily powerful boost to creative activity, although in the first instance only rarely providing opportunities for the execution of projects as real buildings.

A period of 'paper' innovations began. Whole stages in the development of architectural thought culminated in series of unexecuted projects. Tatlin's Monument to the Third International has remained a famous monument of this period, foreshadowing an era of dynamic industrial architecture. But in itself it is a fantasy remote from the practical demands of the difficult war years. In many ways Melnikov prolonged this very line of industrial romance, but he was distinguished by his extraordinary vigour in dealing with practical necessities. Few of the leading Soviet architects of the time built as much as Melnikov – or embodied in brick and glass so many fantastic and paradoxical concepts.

However, his first practical projects were of necessity modest temporary structures in wood. He began with exhibition architecture, a *métier* to which his talent was sympathetic. His inclination towards experiment, towards maximum refinement of architectural form, his acute sense of formal balance, the complex and dynamic way in which he interlocked exterior and interior space in a building – all of these factors gave his pavilions a vigour and expressiveness particularly appropriate to an exhibition context.

The All-Russia Agricultural and Craft Exhibition held in 1923 constituted the first review of Soviet architecture. This provided an opportunity for the public to see in the form of actual buildings what remained of the previous epoch and what was born of the new. As the pavilions were both light and temporary, the architects were able to experiment freely and employ daring ideas.

The pavilion for Makhorka tobacco (one of the less important pavilions) fell to the young Melnikov. It attracted attention, however, and people began to talk about him. The ideas initiated here appeared fully developed two years later in the famous pavilion for the Paris Exhibition of Decorative Arts in 1925. The Parisian pavilion was clearer, cleaner and better proportioned, but its main ideas were already in evidence in 1923. The materials of the earlier pavilion, wood and glass, are simple and traditional but reconsidered with unconventional results. Glass spans the corners and the upper storey is cantilevered; on an exterior corner is inserted a spiral staircase. Simple geometric forms have been combined in a sophisticated complex. As in later works Melnikov here makes great use of inscriptions which run diagonally and employ uneven lettering of differing sizes.

Perhaps the only rival to Melnikov's Soviet pavilion at the 1925 Paris Exhibition of Decorative Art was Le Corbusier's Pavillon de L'Esprit Nouveau. While this was distinguished by a certain logical clarity, Melnikov's aspired to something of the impact of a poster, with its vigorous colours, decorative lettering and emblems, and

89 K. S. Melnikov: Soviet Pavilion, Paris Exhibition of Decorative Art, 1925

expansive composition. The simple volume of the pavilion's rectangular plan was split by diagonal staircases. These abruptly denied the simplicity of the building which to all intents and purposes the architect had already based on the 'logic of the right angle'. Above, the roof-like awnings of the stairs soared like wings, and above that were the letters for USSR in red. For all Melnikov's apparently elementary approach, his buildings reveal a considerable complexity. The staircase was decoratively shaded above by awnings, though not enclosed in the normal sense of the word. It captured within the pavilion the broad flow of external space. Its daring dynamics, the frank simplicity of its materials and the lightness of the pavilion, as well as its rapid erection, stood in contrast to the theatrical monumentality of neighbouring pavilions.

In the latter half of the 1920s the workers' club became a new architectural theme in Melnikov's work. He designed seven clubs between 1927 and 1929, six of which were built. It was a search for a new kind of public building, and together with this a new form of public life; it was a search without tradition and without a clear programme. The 'club' was a major theme of the period, second in priority, perhaps, only to housing. Much was written about clubs at that time, and especially about those designed by Melnikov. They were disturbing, paradoxical and extraordinary, neither familiar nor even alike. Practically beginning afresh each time, Melnikov sought different solutions and never remained content with past achievement.

This is not to say that he was not guided by any principles. Generally, in both the external appearance and the functional construction of the interiors of Melnikov's clubs, there is a system of complex and evolving spatial volumes, by means of which he endeavoured to compose a flexible and multi-purpose environment with minimal expenditure. The auditorium, which in fact occupies a great part of a club's volume, was always planned with due consideration of its possible use in parts, its segmentalization by means of special movable screens into several smaller auditoria. However, technical problems prevented the realization of most of this. The most experimental aspects of the clubs were those which suffered most radically. They were criticized at the time without the fact that they were substantially incomplete being allowed for. His principle of fluid space, which is not related solely to a proposed function but undergoes transformations and develops somewhat freely, was in itself a progressive principle. Here Melnikov is seen to adopt a functional attitude ahead of that of the Constructivists

90

90 K. S. Melnikov: club for workers in the
rubber industry, Moscow, 1927.
Photo: Urs Graf

whose 'functional method' led rapidly towards a fragmentation of
the building by a clear emphasis upon the individual function of
each element.

Melnikov's subsequent structural innovations led to extremely
varied exterior forms which resulted in each case in an unprecedented and spacious solution to the building. Putting aside the
traditional means of articulating the exterior to indicate the social
character of the club (porticos, etc.), Melnikov developed new
means of articulation. Spacious terraces and external staircases are
moved out to cross diagonally in front of the façade. A dynamic

91

organization of the masses of the building is achieved, and emphasis placed upon the entrances and main façade.

    This expression of mass attained its most acute formulation in the Rusakov club where parts of the auditorium project over the façade. These powerful, reinforced-concrete projections drew further criticism from the press. In them were seen both a naïve naturalistic symbolism, in no way a part of Melnikov's architectural ideas, and also, simply, a 'tendency towards formalism'. These reproaches were repeated later when Melnikov's principle of suspending part of the auditorium above the façade had gained a wide acceptance in the designs of other contemporary buildings which required either an auditorium or space for spectators. Perhaps one reason for these attacks in the press was the unexpected

91 K. S. Melnikov: Rusakov Club, Rusakovskaya Ulitsa, Moscow, 1928–29. Photo: Urs Graf

92

92 K. S. Melnikov: Rusakov Club

and extraordinary nature of the expressive means developed by Melnikov and the paradoxical nature of his architectural concepts. Paradox is a characteristic feature of his talent. Both the projections of the Rusakov club and the staircase of the Paris pavilion were paradoxical in their splitting up of rectangular volume, as was the idea for a garage over a bridge in Paris. What was seen as 'formalism' and lack of logic was in fact only the extraordinary use of a strict logic of his own – not only in functional and constructive respects but also in the organization of architectural forms. The chilly appearance of a factory, of smooth surfaces in brick and concrete, of large flat areas of glass in characteristically small frames, were typical of the time and not confined to Melnikov's work. For in the late 1920s and early 1930s a general tendency

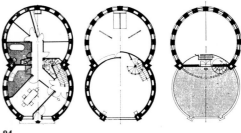

93 94

93 K. S. Melnikov: own house, 1929
94 K. S. Melnikov: own house, 1929, plan

developed among leading architects towards the non-eclectic and the undecorated. It was a kind of romance of industrialism set up against established ideas. All of this helped to unite the principal groups of leftist architecture – OSA and ASNOVA, separated by the cold functionalism of one and the romantic verve of the other. The indefatigable fantasist Melnikov belonged, in effect, to the latter. Besides, there was a certain amount of urban romanticism in the projects of the most austere Constructivists, though they would perhaps be unwilling to recognize this. The strictly functional bases of their most daring aspirations had become law for them. On the other hand an acknowledged aim of maximum attention to aesthetics did not prevent their enemies from ensuring the functional modernity of their own buildings or their economic viability or their rôle in the social organization of public life.

In the years he was working on the clubs, Melnikov designed and built for himself a house on Krivoarbatsky Lane that was very characteristic of his work. It was an experimental house organized according to quite new principles. Two vertical cylinders cut into each other form the basis of the building, which is built of brick but pierced by six-sided spaces which are part solid and part glass. Inside one immediately notices the space rather than the walls, air rather than furnishings. The curvature of the building emphasizes this, as does the dual resolution of the lighting, both in the splintered multitude of small six-sided windows flooding the studio with light from all sides, and the enormous window situated over the entrance porch whereby light flows gently into the living room. In the spacious but shallower bedroom two screens, which extend from floor to ceiling but which are separate from the curved walls, mould the space while lending it a gentle but remarkable fluency of movement.

The handling of space in an artistically expressive manner requiring little volume, and the complete lack of decoration within, brought Melnikov a long series of accusations of formalism and of refusing to consider the practicalities of the building.

The subsequent years of elaboration in architecture were difficult for Melnikov in most respects. Eclecticism brought together architects from very different creative directions while its opponents remained far from united. In fact, it was during the quarrels between the Functionalist–Constructivist faction and those who sought new formal solutions among the ASNOVA group (Melnikov in particular), that the word 'formalism' was first brought into play and joyously seized upon by the eclectics and used against the Constructivists.

Melnikov with his apparent contradictions, his emphatic angularity, the originality of his ideas, and his personal inclination towards fantasy, was among the first to be attacked. This was not because he was insufficiently sensitive to new developments, to the raised-up monumentality and decoration, but because the form of decoration adopted by those architects always proceeded from form to calculation; what were not employed were Melnikov's paradoxical, personal forms.

Commenting at the time on the formal qualities of Melnikov's project for the Narkomtyazhprom building (1934), El Lissitzky wrote: 'Melnikov, who desires at one go to produce the complete building, loads it with such a number of tasteless details and provincialisms that it becomes a disgrace.' ('Forum of Socialist Moscow' *Arkhitektura SSSR* 1935, no. 10.) Unfortunately this was the truth. This project had numerous regrettable features, all of which indicated that working on what was for Melnikov a false basis had in fact transformed his strong qualities – his acute imagination, his willingness to reach extreme conclusions – into weaknesses.

However, the failure of this project did not in fact signify that Melnikov could be written off, or that all of the accusations and attacks on him in the press had been justified. The spirit of artistic experiment, diverted only occasionally from its proper path by prevailing conditions, continued to flourish in his work. As in earlier design work, he emerges often as a pioneer foreshadowing architectural developments of the 1950s and 1960s.

In 1934 he wrote of the unexploited potential of reinforced concrete, and on 'the architectural expression still to be revealed in this most flexible of building materials'. His personal endeavours in this direction, though unrealized in practice, became well known, so that long before post-war Western architects he sensed the plastic richness of reinforced concrete and its constructive possibilities, far outstripping traditional techniques.

A man of vigorous imagination, Melnikov was not content to remain among obstinate champions of a passing stage of architectural thought. He accepted the new challenges and enthusiastically sought a form of expression for that decorative pathos that had become almost law in the art of his time. But even there he went his own way without seeking refuge in a falsely classical theatricality.

His project of 1935 for an apartment house for co-workers of *Izvestia* is most characteristic. This house, with its semicircular balconies, is an architectural utopia. Great cornices, tying the building together, at last form a worthy embellishment. Everything is, in a sense, essential; the unusual aspects of the house are revealed in elements that have a clear functional inspiration, and each solution, as one has come to expect of Melnikov, is unexpected and original.

However, this very originality in formal solutions brings to the fore the fact that the greater number of his projects remained unrealized, together with the important fact that those that were built were far from being his principal or most brilliant works.

(translation John Milner)

This article has been adapted from the Russian essay 'Mel'nikov' by Yu. Gerchuk *Arkhitektura SSSR* No. 8, 1966, pp. 51-5 – EDITOR]

V. N. Semenov

V. N. Beloussov

The stormy years of the twenties which saw the establishment of the Soviet Social State and the destruction of old ideas also saw the foundations of Soviet architecture and the planning and construction of new towns, particularly industrial centres which were to determine future development. The problems of settlements, communal towns, communal flats and houses were studied and experimental building carried out – every effort being directed to mass building. One of the main architects of this period was Vladimir Nikolevich Semenov, professor and member of the USSR Academy of Architecture and Construction, and for many years the head of the Town Building Institute.

Semenov was born in 1874. In 1900 he graduated from the Institute of Civil Engineers in St Petersburg, now the Leningrad Institute of Construction. Like other pioneers, such as Chernyshev, Ilyin and Ivanitsky, he began his work before the Revolution. The first world war interrupted the construction of a garden city for railway workers near Kazan which would have included houses, a hospital and other buildings.

His book *Welfare Planning of Towns*, published in 1912, still surprises one by the boldness of his ideas. He was the first in Russia to approach town planning scientifically. Construction was at the time chaotic, and he stressed the necessity of rigorous planning, flexible zoning and land reserves. It was essential to cater for future alterations in town planning. Extensive researches enabled Semenov to forecast accurately the future development of Russian towns fifty years ahead. For instance, he foresaw the Moscow population growing to six million people. But, under the old régime, his recommendations were ignored.

Semenov regarded the Revolution as a natural development of society and, although he was not a Communist, he always stood for the freedom and independence of the people. He worked in England for several years but, opposed to violence, rushed to the defence of the Boers. His talents and experience were put to the service of the new socialist Russia, and he made a great contribution to the development of the new towns.

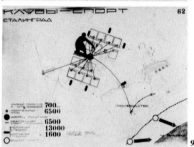

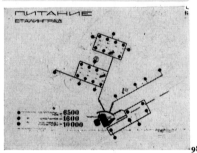

During the first Soviet Five-Year Plan, at the time of hectic industrial development, a group of architects under Professor Semenov at the State Institute of Town Planning, started laying the foundations for socialist towns. In 1929 construction of a large housing area for metal workers began on the Volga around Stalingrad. Semenov and D. M. Sobolev planned to incorporate both industrial and agricultural zones in the new district. They were trying to raise the rural standard of living and to solve the social problem of discrepancies in the working conditions of the rural and urban population, thereby improving the standard of living in country villages and at the same time bringing the town worker closer to nature.

The whole enterprise was planned for 90,000 people, this figure being considered the minimum population essential to the success of the scheme. Further plans were drawn up to provide for the cultural and industrial needs of the locality. Schools for 1600 pupils were envisaged – although such large establishments have, in fact, only appeared in recent times. Schooling was to be closely linked with industrial productivity and agriculture. Medical services would be provided simultaneously for industrial zones, residential districts and rural settlements. Residential areas (in fact micro-areas) were planned to accommodate 6500 people. Services were varied in each neighbourhood. The initial group (800 people),

95 V. Semenov: view of housing estate, Stalingrad, 1929

96 V. Semenov: diagram of the school network in the housing area. Each school is for 1600 children living within a radius of 650 metres.

97 V. Semenov: diagram of the sporting club in the housing area. The central stadium and the Palace of Culture are indicated. The plan includes: club for 700 people; adjoining house; district club for 6500 people; Palace of Culture; district sports field for 6500; area stadium for 13,000; school stadium for 1600; aquatic sports area

98 V. Semenov: diagram for communal feeding arrangements in the housing district. In the centre, kitchens supplying cooked and semi-prepared dishes to dwellings, collective farms and schools

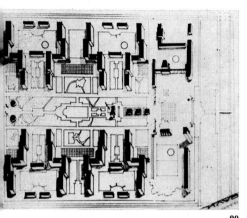

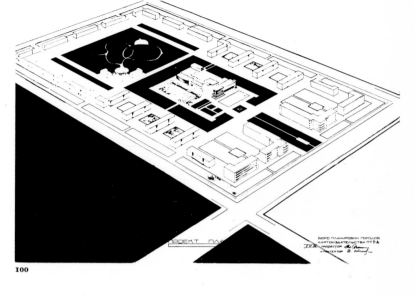

100

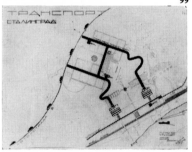

101

for instance, had a common library and rooms for rest and games, while group of living quarters for 1600 people had a communal yard, kindergarten and crêche, sports grounds and cafeteria. Finally, there was to be an entire cultural centre, with sports facilities, restaurant, shops, medical centres, small parks, etc. Several large communities were built on this principle, most of them spreading over an area of one hectare (2.471 acres). Later, several larger ones were built over the original areas, each spread over three hectares instead of one. This project also made provision for easy communication between industrial, living districts and the town centre, situated some kilometres away, and the rest and relaxation zone. Looking ahead, it allowed for fast highways with pedestrian bridges.

Semenov's group suggested that the new town of Losvi (1930) should have communities covering nine hectares and composed of multi-storey buildings, with a park and cultural centre in the middle. The planning was basically the same, great care being given to layout and arrangement of mass. The main access to the central focal point of the complex is accentuated by a large, planned approach. The whole ensemble surrounds the central Palace of Culture.

During the first years of the Soviet Government, Semenov's group concentrated on the problems of urban reconstruction.

102   103

They used to work on simple and obvious principles. These were careful zoning of areas of settlement, relaxation and industry; and making a feature of the Communal Centre. (Semenov used to say 'No centre, no town'.) They further gave attention to access to rivers as, in pre-Revolutionary days, river banks had been ruined by industry, railways and warehouses.

Astrakan is a typical example. The project worked out in 1929 shows convenient zoning, the combination of old buildings with new, larger districts and the creation of a new centre. The central square opens on to the river and the whole construction is orientated in the same fashion. Attention is given to architectural monuments. A group of churches is preserved and emphasized in the new construction.

At the same period, under the direction of Semenov, the plans for a vast health resort were worked out for a Caucasian mineral spa. As always, there were problems. For the first time the foundation was laid for a preventative-medicine complex for the welfare of the working masses. After an extended study of the natural climatic and medical factors, it was possible to put a scheme forward. This involved the planning of sanatoria, rest homes, medical institutions, cultural services, highways, railways, airways, and motor transport.

From 1926 and for the following ten years town building showed an unprecedented impetus. Every year, forty new towns and settlements of a similar type were built.

102 V. Semenov: panorama of the buildings in the centre of Astrakhan, 1929

103 V. Semenov: project 'Kalinin' in Moscow, outlined in the general plan of 1935. It was carried out in 1969 under the supervision of Moscow's chief architect, M. V. Posokhin

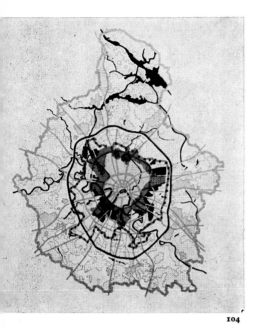

104

The economic factors of industrialization also contributed to the rapid expansion of old towns. Many increased more than three times in size between 1926 and 1939. To give just two examples, Volgagrad grew from 151,000 to 445,000 inhabitants and Novosibirsk from 120,000 to 644,000. Such expansion, naturally, necessitated an army of experienced builders. The State Institute took charge of urban projects, the general planning of new industrial centres and the reconstruction of old towns.

In 1932 a competition was announced to study new planning ideas and examine various proposals such as a suggestion to move Moscow to another site. This competition, aimed at solving the problem of the development of Moscow, was organized by the Monovet Administration of Architectural Planning under the supervision of Semenov. With the help of many talented Soviet architects he worked out a general plan for the capital, combining new principles with the traditions of ancient Russian town building. The scheme preserved the most essential of Moscow's historic foundations, but also introduced radical changes in keeping with the times. It envisaged an increase of population from 3·7 million to 5 million. The capital was to be enlarged at the expense of reserved land from 28,500 hectares to 60,000 hectares, with new highways. The roads were to be widened from 16 to 18 metres and from 50 to 60 metres. Parks were laid out from the outskirts to the centre and work was continued on the Metro.

During the second world war Semenov was at the head of the Town Building Institute of the USSR Academy of Architecture. He worked on settlement projects for Simbirsk and middle Asia. His work, which entailed the study of local climatic conditions, available resources and war-time requirements was, to a great extent, responsible for the distribution of new industries in the Far East.

After the last war, working on a project for the reconstruction of Rostov, Semenov formulated important practical solutions for the expansion of Soviet towns.

(translation Elizabeth Heath)

N. A. Ladovsky 1881-1941

S. O. Khan-Mahomedov

105

Nikolai Aleksandrovich Ladovsky was one of the most influential of Soviet architects of the 1920s. He was the leader of the Rationalist movement.

Even before receiving a specialized architectural training, he spent years studying design, taking part in and winning prizes in many competitions. In 1914 he became a student of the Moscow College of Painting, Sculpture and Architecture and eventually qualified as an architect.

In 1920 he became a lecturer at VKHUTEMAS and there worked out a new basic course. He encouraged his students to work as individuals, using their intuition. He considered it important that they should develop a sense of fantasy, and stimulated their imaginations by showing them how to organize space in three dimensions. They experimented with rhythm and colour. They started with abstract two-dimensional exercises, moving gradually to the study of volume and space. In his senior classes, where more practical results were expected, his skill emphasized the wonderful complexity of possible solutions, suggesting that none were final, each having its merits. The work of his students was particularly bold and original. As leader of the Rationalist movement, ASNOVA (the New Association of Architects), Ladovsky was committed to

106   107

105 N. A. Ladovsky

106 Exercise in the representation of structure (cantilever) 1921 (course I), designed by S. A. Lopakina under the tutorship of Ladovsky at VKHUTEMAS

107 Exercise in the representation of the formal qualities of mass and equilibrium 1922 (basic course) by A. Arkin under the tutorship of N. A. Ladovsky at VKHUTEMAS

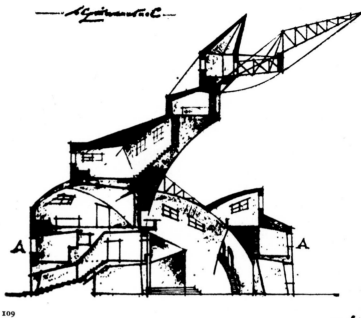

108

108, 109 N. Ladovsky: design for a commune, plan and section, 1920

109

110

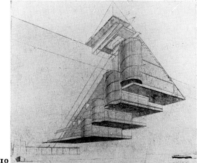

111

112

113

110 Exercise in the representation of the formal qualities of mass and equilibrium: pier and restaurant suspended over a lake, 1922 (course II), by Simbirchev under the tutorship of N. A. Ladovsky at VKHUTEMAS

111, 112 Exercises in the representation of dynamism, rhythm, etc. 1923: top I. V. Lamtsov, bottom M. A. Turkus, both under the tutorship of N. A. Ladovsky at VKHUTEMAS

113 Study in the representation of solid and void, tower for the manufacture of alkaline solutions, 1922 (course II), designed by I. Gruschenko under the tutorship of Ladovsky at VKHUTEMAS

formulating his beliefs. One of the most difficult problems facing
an architect, he believed, was the ability of man to orientate himself
in space. The laws of perspective distorted forms; it was the
business of the architect to preserve the essential characteristics of
geometrical forms and to imbue them with art. In his laboratory at
VKHUTEMAS he built a number of devices for judging spatial
characteristics, properties of form and volume, etc.

During his first year as a lecturer at VKHUTEMAS he designed one
of the first housing estates (or communes) – a group of multi-storey
buildings enclosing a court, and linked by stair-wells. He entered
many competitions – that for the Smolensk market in Moscow
(1920); the memorial to Columbus in Santa-Domingo (1923); the
Soviet pavilion at the Paris Exhibition of 1925; the Mosps theatre
in Moscow (1931); a theatre in Sverdlovsk (1931); and the Palace
of the Soviets, Moscow (1931–32).

Ladovsky's ideas on town planning and prefabricated dwellings,
which he designed in detail, were of considerable interest. The
pre-fabrication systems he proposed for Moscow and Ivanovo in
the mid-twenties were, however, unusually complicated. In 1927
he drew up a plan for Kostino, an industrial town near Moscow
with 25,000 inhabitants. Mindful of the new impetus given to
industrial development, he divided his town into three distinct
zones, each of which could expand without impinging on the other
– an industrial area, a housing area and a park with a social centre.

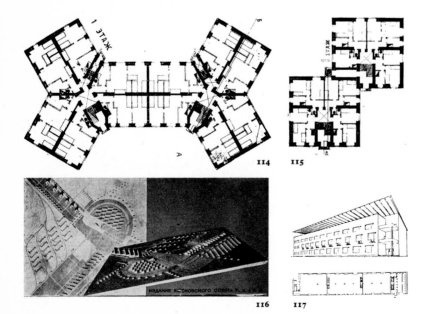

114 115

116 117

114–117 N. Ladovsky: details of housing
and layout for the industrial settlement of
Kostino, 1927

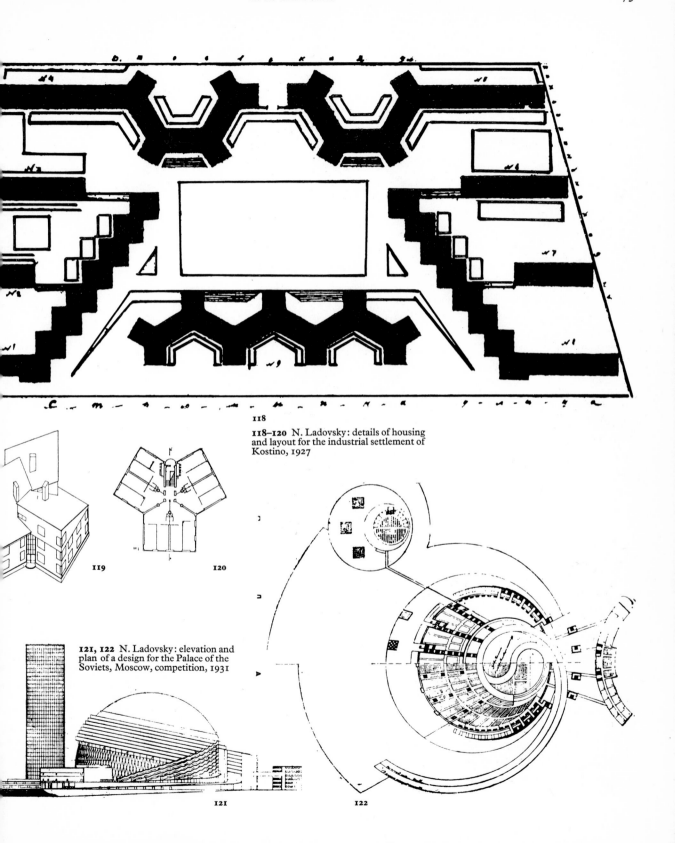

118

118–120 N. Ladovsky: details of housing and layout for the industrial settlement of Kostino, 1927

119   **120**

121, 122 N. Ladovsky: elevation and plan of a design for the Palace of the Soviets, Moscow, competition, 1931

121   **122**

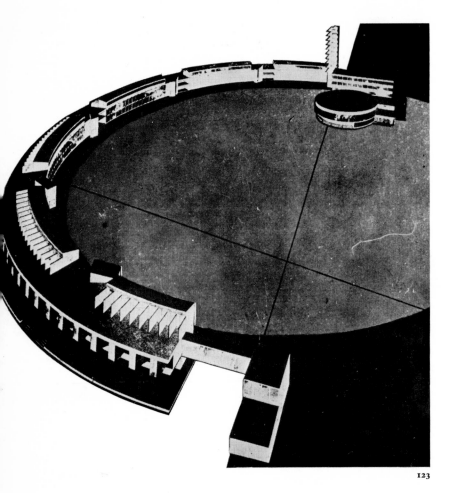

123–127 N. Ladovsky: layout and designs
for individual buildings for a 'garden city'
competition, 1930

123

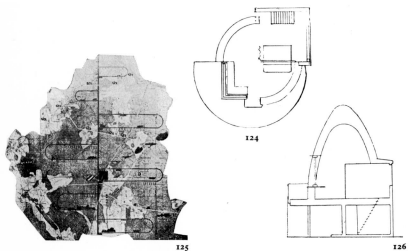

124

125

126

127

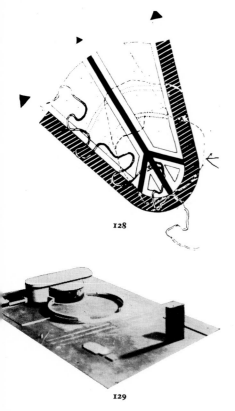

128 N. Ladovsky: basic diagram for a town
laid out as a parabola, 1930
129 N. Ladovsky: model of a theatre for
Sverdlovsk, competition, 1931

In 1928 Ladovsky and a group of supporters resigned from
ASNOVA and founded ARU (The Association of Urban Architects).
They were interested mainly in the planning of new areas, factory
towns and large housing estates. Similarly, Ladovsky's group at
VKHUTEMAS had broken away to form VKHUTEIN and were, at the
end of the twenties, busily designing new towns. Two of these
projects of 1928 are noteworthy: V. Lavrov's linear town and T.
Varentsov's design for a radial town with ring roads. Ladovsky
carefully considered the merits of each, then in 1930 he drew up
a plan of his own which might be regarded as a reminiscence of
Milyutin's famous plan. It was, in any event, a rejection of the
traditional radial plan. His layout was a compromise, based on a
parabola, with the three main zones – industry, housing and
leisure – lying on its axis. He wished to apply this pattern to Moscow, taking as the main axis the line of Gorky and Leningrad
Streets. The scheme was first published in 1930, together with a
series of justificatory articles. But it was not much favoured,
though in time – at the end of the fifties – it was to be rediscovered
by Constantinos Doxiades and renamed Dynapolis.

In 1930 Ladovsky prepared plans in competition for a 'garden
city' outside Moscow, to be linked to the capital by a complex of
motorways running parallel, all allowing for different speeds. The
town was to be erected by methods of prefabrication, all housing
units to be factory-made and to be rapidly assembled on prepared
sites. The details of such a system occupied him until well into the
thirties.

(translation Kate Hunloke)

G. B. Barkhin 1880-1969

M. G. Barkhin

Grigory Borisovich Barkhin was born at Perm in the Urals. His childhood was spent in the far east of Siberia on a housing estate attached to the vast smelting works of Zabaykalsk, founded in the reign of Peter the Great. He started work there at the age of ten, and taught himself draughtsmanship and graphic design in the works' office. His remarkable talent for drawing was noticed and the Siberian Society sent him to study in St Petersburg. He had to travel to European Russia on horseback, because there was no railway in Siberia at the time. In 1908 he graduated as an architect from the Petersburg Academy of Arts. The training at the Academy – the oldest architectural school in the country – was classical in form and in spirit. But in his final thesis 'A Necropolis near a Metropolis', he showed his dissatisfaction with the old rules. He made detailed designs for a large temple in the style of the architect Gruzy, an exponent of a popular southern vernacular style. It is difficult to imagine why he should have chosen such a source of inspiration, for it is evident in his designs for rooms in the Museum of Fine Arts in Moscow – the Egyptian lobby, the Egyptian, Assyrian and Greek halls, the Roman *thermae*, the Renaissance court and others – that he had an exceptional knowledge of the more acceptable historical styles. He also did research at Irkutsk into the character of early Russian classicism. He designed and built the rotunda and semicircular colonnade for the tomb of Yusupov in Moscow, the new Moscow University building on Manezhny Square, and, among other small items, the cast-iron and bronze mouldings and obelisks for the Borodinsky bridge.

At this time, industrial architecture was grimly utilitarian – partly because of a lack of basic materials. During the early years of the first world war he designed a range of munitions factories, and this activity perhaps conditioned the change from his pre-war style to that of the post-Revolutionary period.

He was already practising in Moscow before the Revolution, but on his return to Moscow in 1919 he plunged enthusiastically into the task of rebuilding the country and developing a new Soviet architecture. He rebuilt hospitals in Moscow and housing for those working on the Sormovsky hydro-electric power station, building

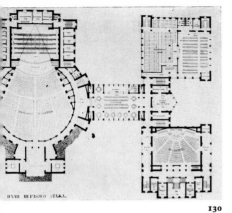

two- and four-roomed flats in an unassuming style, with contrasting white walls and red-tile roofs. He was then entrusted with the planning of a model state farm for grain production, and the appropriateness of his organization and individual building design was so admired that it was adopted for other state and collective farms and villages (the *sovkhoz* and *kolkhoz*). In 1920 he focused on theoretical work, writing two books devoted to the construction of housing: *Housing Estates and Gardens for Workers* and *Contemporary Housing Estates*, in which he considered a house, not as a separate entity, but as part of a total complex, linked to nature. His work on cheap housing during the years when Soviet Russia had barely emerged from the civil war was seminal. In 1922 he also wrote a teaching manual.

Barkhin's most active years were those from 1924 to the second world war. This period covered two phases in Soviet architecture – from 1920 to 1933 innovations were made in Functionalism and Constructivism, resulting in a degree of formalism in architecture; thereafter, beginning effectively with the competition for the Palace of Soviets in Moscow, a reappraisal was made of the 'classical inheritance'. The psychological validity of this change in architecture is not yet fully understood; basically architects were asked to reassess the old aesthetic values of architecture. This reappraisal disturbed Barkhin more than most of his contemporaries. After 1933 he concentrated only on town planning.

From the twenties onwards, Barkhin worked with his eldest son, Mikhail, also an architect. The partnership began when Mikhail was a student and lasted for twenty-five years.

The twenties were a period of sweeping change. Relatively little was built, but a great deal designed, and a new spirit was evident in the projects. Architects were trying to express the spirit of the great Revolution in architectural form. New socialist aspirations were formulated to meet the changed demands of society. The workers needed new housing, clubs, factories, villages and towns. The new concept had a single purpose – to break down the old architectural norms and to establish new ones.

One of Barkhin's earliest designs – a municipal centre for the city of Ivanovo – was successful in competition and completed in

130, 131 G. Barkhin: municipal centre, Ivanovo, 1924, plan and elevation

1924. This included a theatre (1,250 seats), an assembly hall (400 seats), a Lenin museum, a library, a gymnasium, rooms for meetings, and a canteen. The individual elements were clearly expressed in the plan. The volumes were given clear-cut and contrasting

132

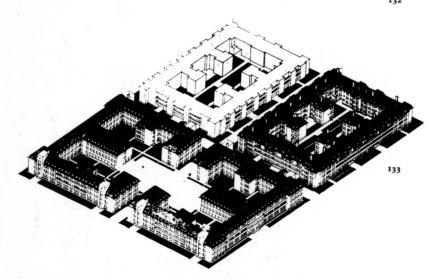

133

cubic and cylindrical forms. Later Barkhin also designed housing for Ivanovo. During this period he prepared even more ambitious designs for the competition for the Palace of Culture at Dnepropetrovsk. The architectural forms were handled with greater lightness on this occasion, but the principles embodied were the same as those used in earlier designs. Traditional stalls and balconies were rejected for the theatre; instead an amphitheatre was proposed – a form subsequently adopted by many architects designing theatres.

In 1925 Barkhin prepared drawings for the printing plant and offices for *Izvestia* on Pushkin Square, Moscow. The offices overlook the Square, the printing works are at the rear. Two variants were produced – the first with a tower was rejected, the second with an almost square façade set on *pilotis* was accepted. The static

132 G. Barkhin: Palace of Culture, Dnepropetrovsk, 1925, elevation
133 G. Barkhin: housing, Ivanovo, 1927, axonometric
134 G. Barkhin: post office, Kharkov, 1927, perspective

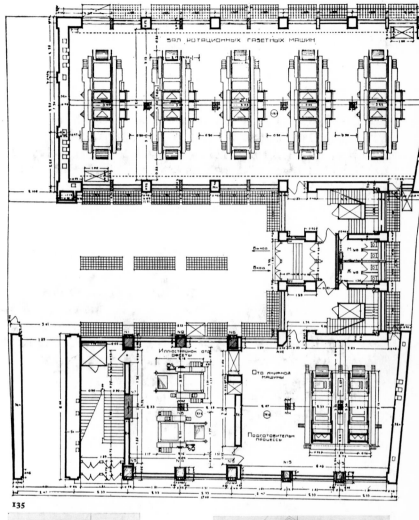

135

136

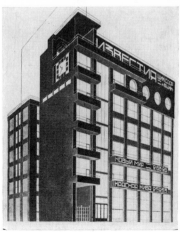

137

135 G. Barkhin: *Izvestia* building,
Moscow, 1925, plan

136 G. Barkhin: *Izvestia* building, Moscow,
1925, variant I

137 G. Barkhin: *Izvestia* building, Moscow,
1925, variant II

138

quality of the square, however, was countered with a more dynamic extension along Gorky Street, and the introduction of an array of projecting balconies. Part of the façade screening the services was left blank and some of the windows on the sixth floor were rounded. Giant lettering was added to the top and first floor levels. The design was both robust and unorthodox; it was greatly admired when it was first completed and still arouses interest today.

138 G. Barkhin: *Izvestia* building, Moscow, 1927
139 G. Barkhin: *Izvestia* building, Moscow

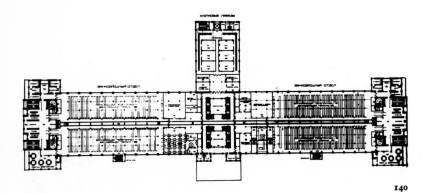

140

140 G. Barkhin: textile factory, Ivanovo, 1926, plan

At the end of the twenties, Barkhin planned several institutions for further education, the most interesting of which is the car manufacturers' club, next to the car factory in Gorky. This beautifully thought-out design allowed for extension and flexibility in the arrangement of the individual rooms and the large hall. Only a part, unfortunately, was built.

Barkhin was always intrigued by theatre design. Two of his demand particular attention, one for Rostov-on-Don, which he won in competition in 1930, and one that he built in 1932 in Sverdlovsk. The Rostov project has an auditorium with 2500 seats, a concert hall for 800, exhibition halls, and club rooms. The Sverdlovsk plan included a great flexible space which could serve as a theatre for 4000, an assembly hall for 6000, or, when the stage is lowered and included in the floor area, for 8000. A theatre was also included

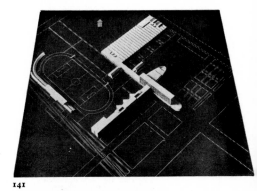

141

141 G. Barkhin: car manufacturing plant, Gorky, 1928, model

142, 143 G. Barkhin: theatre for Rostov-on-Don, 1930, plan and model

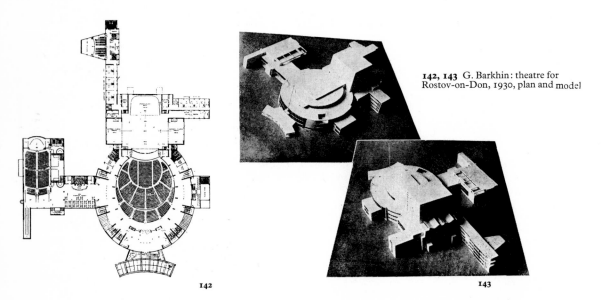

142   143

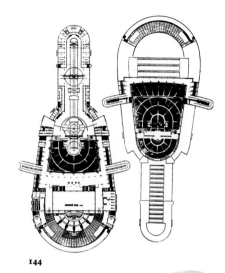

144

146a

146b

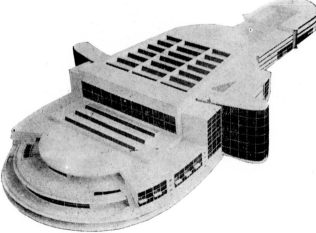

145

144, 145 G. Barkhin: design for a synthetic theatre seating 8000, Sverdlovsk, 1932, plan and model

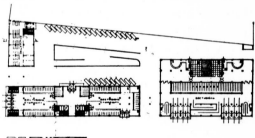

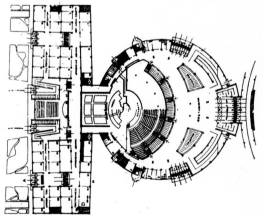

146, 147 G. Barkhin: Palace of Labour, Moscow, 1933, plan and perspective

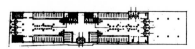

147

in the Place of Labour that Barkhin designed in the mid-thirties for the Moscow Council of Professional Unions; on this occasion it had only 2000 seats. This low conference hall was set against a fourteen-storey office block. Finally, in 1947, Barkhin published a theoretical and historical survey of theatre design, *The Architecture of the Theatre.*

Other buildings of his Constructivist period include spinning mills, a printing works for the Azerbaijan state publishing house in Baku and a post office for Kharkov.

Barkhin's next phase of activity was distinguished by his plans for Moscow (1933–7) and the rebuilding of Sevastopol (1944–7). In Moscow he headed the group of planners and architects responsible for the Dzerzhinsky sector, a considerable area stretching north–south for more than twenty kilometres. In the northern part of this area he joined a number of isolated open spaces to form one large park, extending almost to the walls of the Kremlin. Major routes and transport links were determined, and housing layouts drawn, but only part of the total was implemented. As far as Sevastopol was concerned, when he arrived there in the spring of 1944, he found little more than the charred ruins of the old city. He was thus able to make far-reaching proposals: all stores and warehouses were to be moved away from the old waterfront, opening the new city out to the sea; the eighteenth-century street grid was to be discarded and the promontory in the centre of town made the focus for a new system of streets and ring roads; the 'heroic' character of the town was to be emphasized. His plan was not fully realized, but those parts which were completed gave life to both the surviving historic areas and the newly-built areas.

Another of his late works was the layout for a large area south-west of Moscow for the International Exhibition of 1967, done in conjunction with members of the Architectural Institute, Moscow. For forty-five years he taught at this Institute, respected and greatly loved by his students. This perceptive and generous man died at the age of ninety on 11 April 1969, just as this article was being completed.

(translation Kate Hunloke)

148

148 G. Barkhin: model of the proposed rebuilding of Sevastopol, 1944–47

N. A. Milyutin 1889-1942

S. O. Khan-Mahomedov

Nikolai Aleksandrovich Milyutin was one of the most influential architectural theorists in the first half of the 1930s, as a result of the publication of his two principal works, *The Planning of Socialist Towns* (*Sotsgorod*, 1933) and *Essential Questions of Theory in Soviet Architecture* (1933).

Milyutin's childhood was spent in St Petersburg and the country. From 1905 to 1912 he attended an art school, earning his living at the same time. He played an active part in trade-union and revolutionary movements, was a member of the Bolshevik party, and thus took part in the October revolution. During the 1920s he held several Government posts (Assistant Commissar, Commissar and Member of the Small Commissariat of the RSFSR).

By the end of the 1920s town planning was the major subject of discussion in architectural circles. As president of the State Commission on the planning of the new towns, Milyutin was deeply involved in these discussions; he made a careful study of most town-planning projects, read all the literature on the subject and analysed the various solutions, particularly those relating to housing problems. His friend Ginsburg was a great influence on him.

His own considered views were outlined in *Sotsgorod*. Between 1930 and 1935 he was president of the Socialist Resettlement Committee and the Housing Academy; from 1931 to 1934 he edited the journal *Soviet Architecture* (*Sovietskaya Arkhitektura*).

For Milyutin, the reorganization of the workers' lives necessarily implied new social services and arrangements. Women were to be freed from domestic drudgery, sanitary conditions were to be improved and all new building was to be properly planned. But having acted as head of the People's Commissariat of Finance of the RSFSR, he was only too well aware that the workers' standard of living could not be changed without constant reference to the general financial state. All his proposals for higher standards were thus based on economic considerations.

His prime interest in planning was to break down the distinctions between town and country living. Industry, he thought, should be closely related to all new settlements; but there should be a balanced relationship. He did not want factories to act as the focus of a few scattered housing estates, nor to be carefully segregated – the workers living in garden cities far from their working quarters. His particular solution was a linear city unit, illustrated in *Sotsgorod*, which could be threaded even through old towns.

His linear city was a variation of those of Soria y Mata, Levi, Okhtovich and Leonidov, but was more intricately developed. Factories and dwellings were placed, broadly, in parallel zones, allowing both proximity and room for virtually unrestricted expansion. In detail, he proposed six, strictly controlled, parallel strips:

1 railways
2 factories, workshops, stores as well as research institutes and technical colleges
3 green belt with a main highway running through it
4 a residential zone in three sections: public and communal buildings, municipal offices, canteens and clinics; housing; and finally, children's hostels, kindergartens and crèches
5 park with sports facilities, playing fields, swimming pools, etc.
6 an agricultural zone with gardens, allotments, dairy farms, etc.

Ideally, he would have liked a lake or river in the park as an extension to the leisure facilities and even as an alternative route of transportation.

He embodied his principles in three concrete proposals – plans for Magnitogorsk, the Stalingrad tractor factory and the Gorki car plant. When planning these towns he took for granted a new social organization. As far as possible everything was to be collectivized and women regarded as equal to men. Certainly they were to work as equals. Families, as such, were to be abolished. Adults were to be housed separately, in individual adjoining cells – though inter-leading doors were to be provided for intimate contact, when occasion might demand. 'Home' life was to be replaced by community life, individual kitchens by canteens; repair shops, work-rooms, laundries, schools and crèches would be shared by all.

Unlike other architects engaged in designing similar communal residences, Milyutin considered that the individual cells should be used for study and leisure and also for the storage and display of private possessions, though these should be kept to the minimum (the cells were made tiny in order to ensure this).

He designed two alternative schemes for a three-storey residential unit for 400–800 people, complete with canteens, libraries, and other facilities. The residential cells all overlooked the woods and fields of the green belt. Similarly, the windows of the individual houses that he planned were all designed to open on one side, though he did, on occasion, plan houses in parallel rows, with a 75 to 100 metre space between. The three-storey residential blocks were to be built as cheaply as possible, using mainly timber, with a timber framework devised by himself and as little brick as possible. A prototype was put up in Moscow.

During the middle and late thirties Milyutin developed his ideas further. In 1940, already an established authority and a government official of long standing, he decided to sit as an external student for the state examination of the Moscow Architectural Institute. His thesis proposed a flyover for Moscow and he was awarded an architectural degree on its merits.

During the last years of his life, he concentrated on proposals for new towns, but the war and his failing health prevented the realization of any of these.

(translation Marina Corby)

M. Ya. Ginsburg 1892-1946

S. O. Khan-Mahomedov

Moisei Yakovlevich Ginsburg played an important part in the development of Soviet architecture, both as a theoretician and as a practising architect. He was the son of an architect in Minsk. While still at school he studied with a local artist and helped his father. His school education completed, he travelled abroad and enrolled at the Academy of Arts, Milan. He graduated there in 1914 and returned to Russia. During the war he studied at the Rizhsky Polytechnic, Moscow, and three years after was awarded a second degree, this time in engineering. His first commission was for a private house in Eupatoria, the Crimea.

In 1921 he moved to Moscow and took up teaching. In 1923, he became a professor at VKHUTEMAS, heading the faculty of the history of architecture and architectural theory. At the same time he taught at the Moscow Institute of Higher Technology and established himself as an active member of the Russian Academy of Artistic Studies (RAKHN).

In 1923 he published his first theoretical work, *Rhythm in Architecture*. In the same year two of his articles, 'Old and New' and 'Contemporary Aesthetics', were printed in *Architecture*; in them he set down the credo of Constructivism. From 1923 to 1924 he was active in Moscow architectural circles, giving a series of lectures at RAKHN on contemporary trends and publishing this analysis in 1924 in a book, *Style and the Epoch* – another Constructivist manifesto. His project for a 'Palace of Labour', entered in competition in 1923, reflected his somewhat romantic ideas of symbolism at this time. As one of the chief editors of the newly established review *Contemporary Architecture*, he wrote a whole series of theoretical articles, developing a programme for the new architecture.

In contrast to the theoretical works written during the first half of the 1920s, devoted mainly to the fundamental problems of architectural composition and style, these articles focused rather on functional design and on social problems.

During these years, Ginsburg completed a number of projects, mainly for competitions – the Textile building, the covered market,

149

150

149 Moisei Yakovlevich Ginsburg
150 M. Ginsburg: Palace of Labour, Moscow, competition, 1923, perspective

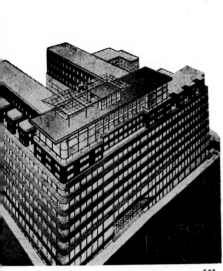

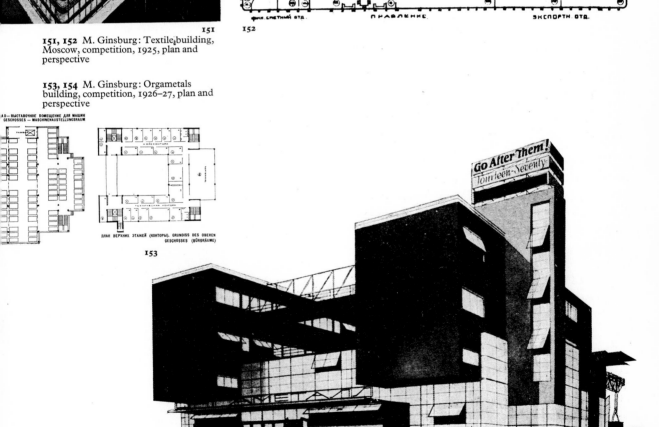

151, 152 M. Ginsburg: Textile building, Moscow, competition, 1925, plan and perspective

153, 154 M. Ginsburg: Orgametals building, competition, 1926–27, plan and perspective

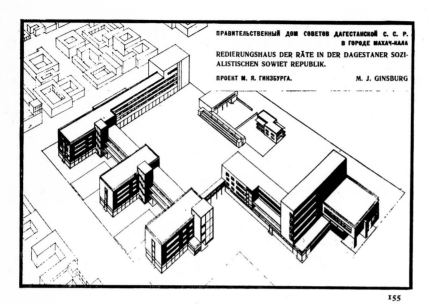

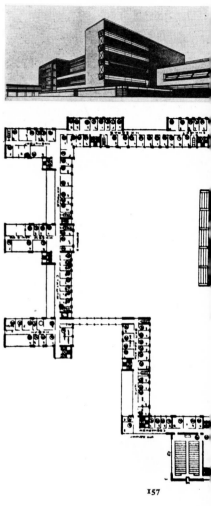

155

the Orgametals building, Rusgetorg in Moscow, a House of the Soviets in Machachkala, and a Court of Justice in Alma-Ata. These projects give evidence of a new style – an attempt to give form to functional ideas incorporating modern materials. One or two of these designs were built – for example the Court of Justice in Alma-Ata.

But Ginsburg considered that one of the most important problems for Soviet architects was to solve the problems of housing. In 1926 in a design for the Malaya Bronna, Moscow, he proposed five-storey flats with related service buildings. In a competition the following year he designed a housing estate with a variety of individual flats, set around a communal block containing a nursery school, club, dining room, etc. Between 1928 and 1932 a group of architects under the leadership of Ginsburg worked on the resolution of similar programmes. They worked first on a site near Stroikoma, RSFSR, planning one of the first really large-scale housing estates. They concentrated on the design of economic dwellings, allowing each family a flat of its own – a real possibility in those days. Five experimental blocks were eventually built, the greatest interest being stimulated by that on Novinsky Avenue, Moscow, put up between 1928 and 1929. There were to have been four independent elements – dwellings, a community building, a service building and a children's unit – all linked by enclosed corridors. The whole, however, was never completed.

157

155–7 M. Ginsburg: House of Soviets, Machachkala, 1926, plan and perspectives

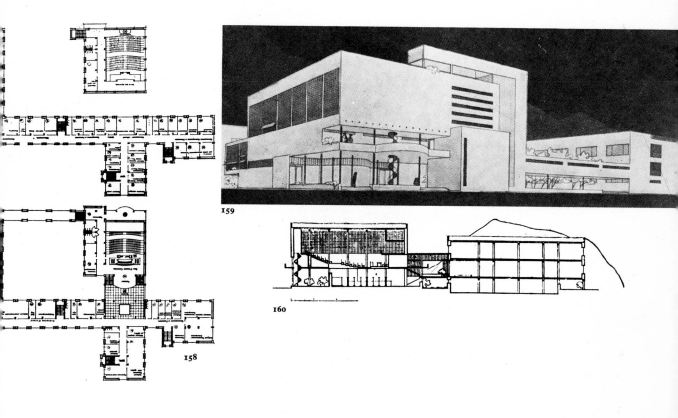

159

160

158

161

158–161 M. Ginsburg: House of Justice,
Alma-Ata (now State University of
Kazakhstan), 1927–30

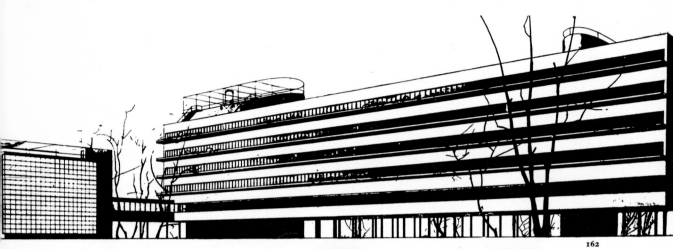

162

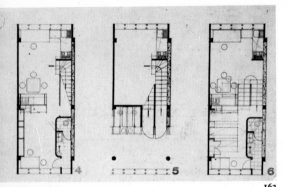

163

164

165

162–166 M. Ginsburg: Housing on
166   Novinsky Boulevard, Moscow, 1928–29

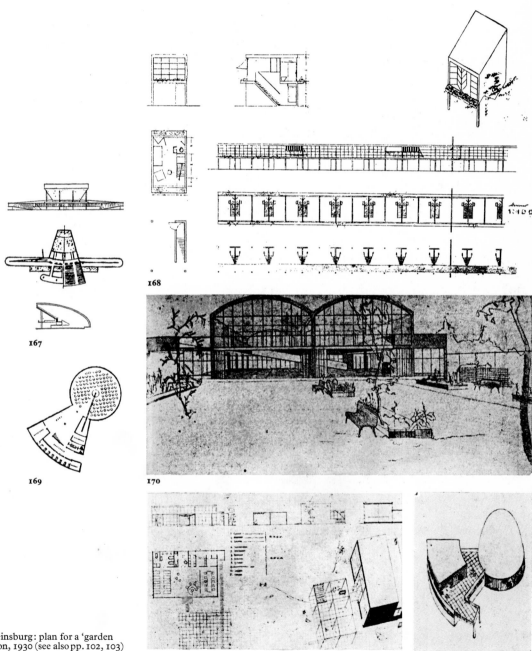

167–171 M. Ginsburg: plan for a 'garden
city' competition, 1930 (see also pp. 102, 103)

Ginsburg's group worked next within the RSFSR state plan for socialist resettlement which involved problems of regional planning (such as their designs for the Cherikovsky industrial region). The plan for 'Green City', a garden city prepared by Ginsburg in association with Barshch, was considered particularly provocative. For a suburb of Moscow they proposed rows of independent houses, set among trees, strung out along the roads.

During the early thirties, Ginsburg directed a large group of architects in the preparation of a regional plan for the south coast of the Crimea, followed by a detailed study of the Yalta–Mishkov–Alupka region, a plan which was regarded as the first of its sort to be entirely rationally worked out.

Ginsburg was at his best when working in a group; he was a lively man and a good organizer. For years he was the focus of a flexible group, most of whose members had been active in OSA during the 1920s – M. Barshch, V. Vladimirov, A. Pasternak, G. Zundblat, I. Leonidov, G. Vegman, I. Milinis and others. Together they worked on housing and planning studies in the Crimea, and were responsible also for sanatoria in Kislovodsk.

Ginsburg entered several competitions by himself; during the 1930s he prepared drawings for the Palace of the Soviets and the Nemirovich-Danchenko theatre in Moscow, a theatre in Sverdlosk, a Park of Culture and Rest in Moscow, the Soviet pavilion at the Paris International Exhibition in 1937, the *Izvestia* building and the Narkomtyazhprom building in Moscow. He also worked independently on plans for hostels for 'Krasny Kamen' in Nizhny Tagil and the park on Mount David in Tbilisi.

Meanwhile, he was also continuing with his theoretical work. In 1934 he published *Housing* and wrote a critique of eclecticism and mere stylistic application, urging his contemporaries to study the problems of standardization.

He acted as editor at the Academy of Architecture for a large-scale *General History of Architecture* and during the war he headed a committee on prefabrication. He was concerned in particular with the problems of rebuilding Sevastopol. He drew numerous plans for the central area, trying to preserve its historical core. But he did not finish this project. Nor did he complete his sanatoria in Kislovodsk and Oreanda in the Crimea – though they were built after his death to an altered plan and with 'enriched' exteriors. During his last year, he began a great treatise on architecture, but he finished only one section, that on 'Tectonics'.

(translation Kate Hunloke)

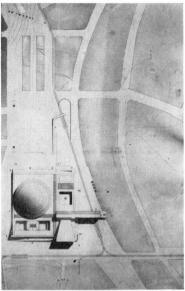

172–174 M. Ginsburg: Palace of the Soviets, Moscow, competition 1932, plan and model

M. Barshch

V. Khazanova

The first number of *Contemporary Architecture*, the journal of the Contemporary Association of Architects, was published in 1928. Among several score of permanent contributors were the names of two students from VKHUTEMAS – Mikhail Barshch and Mikhail Sinyavsky. For three months the journal published their joint diploma project, 'The Central Food Market in Bolotnoi Square, Moscow'. In this elegant design, directly influenced by Functionalism and Constructivism, the circulation patterns were carefully thought out. Horizontal buildings and three skyscrapers were coordinated to form an impressive whole. Two new names thus entered the history of Soviet architecture. But it was rather the construction of the Moscow planetarium (1927–29) that brought fame to the two young architects. It was a new type of institution, designed not only for scientific purposes, but also for the entertainment of the people.[1] Aleksei Gan, the ideologist of Constructivism, described it as a theatre without actors, in which men serve science by presenting it optically with the aid of complicated equipment.[2]

175 M. Barshch and M. Sinyavsky: diploma project for the central food market in Moscow, VKHUTEMAS 1926

БАРЩ И СИНЯВСКИЙ. ЦЕНТРАЛЬНЫЙ ПРОДОВОЛЬСТВЕННЫЙ РЫНОК. ДИПЛОМНЫЕ ПРОЕКТЫ ВХУТЕМАС. ВАРИАНТ Д PLAN GRUNDRISS
BARTSCH UND SINJAVSKY. ENTWURFE EINES MARKTHALLE

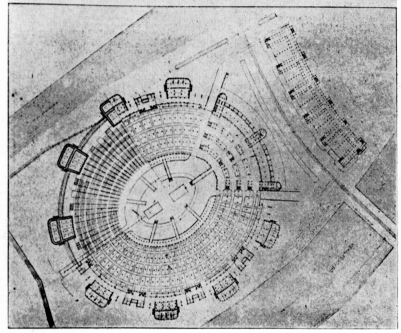

176

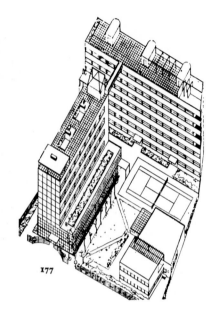

177

Inspired by Le Corbusier, these two architects worked with Burov on a design for a House of Industry in Sverdlovsk. However, from 1929 onwards Barshch and Sinyavsky started working separately. Sinyavsky worked under Ginsburg on new housing projects connected with socialist planning, while, also under Ginsburg's direction, Barshch, V. Vladimirov, I. Milinis, S. Orlovsky, A. Pasternak, and L. Slavina concentrated on the development of a living unit for the future, a complex of residential and communual quarters, linked by covered passages. Such a prototype[3] was built successfully in Moscow on the Gogol Boulevard. From 1929 to 1930 the Association of Contemporary Architects concentrated on communal housing and services, thus giving form to early social utopias.

Barshch and Vladimirov planned a 'communal house' for 1000 adults in one unit and 680 children in two additional units, sub-divided according to their schooling. There were separate cubicles with showers, built-in cupboards, a table and folding bed, also a library and reading room, work rooms, etc. This project, though

176 M. Barshch and M. Sinyavsky: diploma project for the central food market in Moscow, VKHUTEMAS 1926

177 M. Barshch, V. Vladimirov, I. Milinis, S. Orlovsky, A. Pasternak and L. Slavina: RJSKT demonstration project, Gogol Boulevard, no. 8, Moscow, 1928–29

178

179

180

178–180 M. Barshch and M. Sinyavsky:
Moscow planetarium, 1929

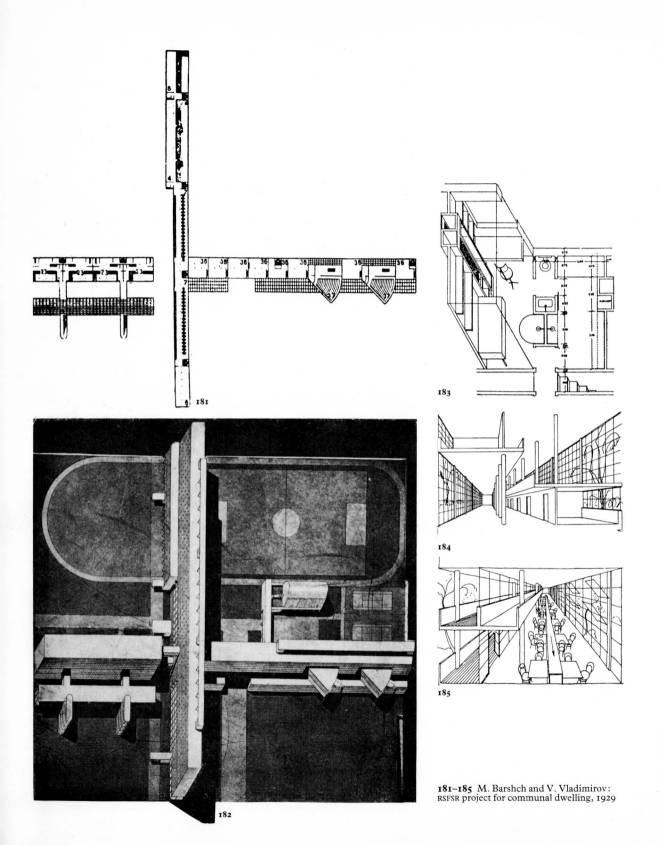

181–185 M. Barshch and V. Vladimirov:
RSFSR project for communal dwelling, 1929

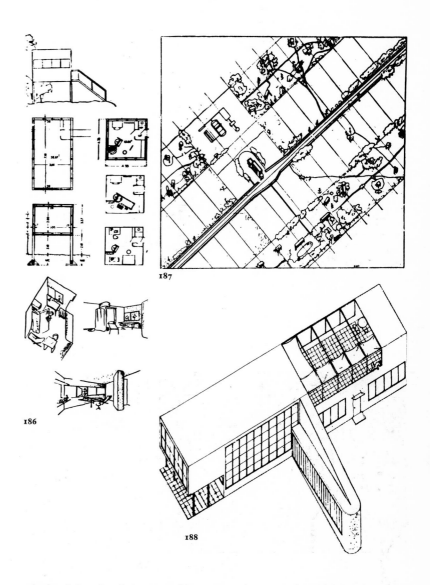

187

186

188

186 M. Barshch, V. Vladimirov,
M. Ohitovitch, N. Sokolov, and
N. Vorotyntseva: project for Magnitogorsk,
single living unit, 1929

187 M. Barshch, V. Vladimirov,
M. Ohitovitch, N. Sokolov and
N. Vorotyntseva: project for socialist
housing estate in Magnitogorsk, principles
of settlement

188 M. Barshch, V. Vladimirov,
M. Ohitovitch, N. Sokolov, and
N. Vorotyntseva: project for Magnitogorsk,
community building (set at intervals of a
kilometre)

admired in the late twenties, was subsequently criticized by its designers as limited and restricted.[4]

While he elaborated plans for Magnitogorsk together with his colleagues Vladimirov, Ohitovitch, Pavlov, Pasternak, Vorotyntseva, Kalinin, Savinov and Schmidt, Barshch was preoccupied with personal relationships within the collective units. He also worked with Ginsburg on the project for 'Green City'.

Ginsburg planned projects to solve the problems of socialist rehousing.[5] He advocated fighting for a socialist identity, providing for its development and bringing man closer to nature,[6] made by

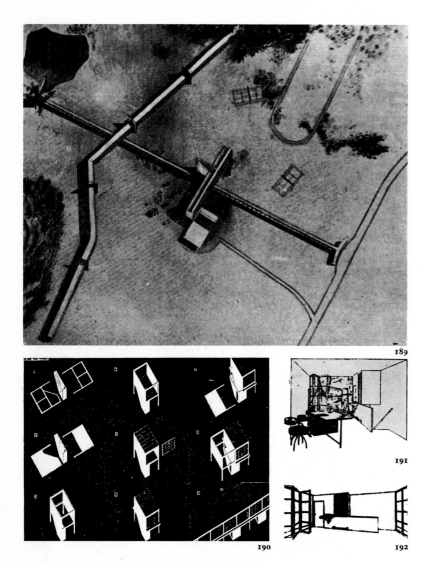

189

190   192

191

189 M. Barshch and M. Ginsburg: project
for Green City, near Moscow, section of
settlement, 1930
190-192 M. Barshch and M. Ginsburg:
project for Green City, a living unit, 1930

man, for the sake of man. While life in such communal dwellings
was strictly regulated, it was possible to form free associations.[7]

The buildings in Magnitogorsk were surrounded by space,
greenery, light and sun, and free from all the constrictions of town
life.[8] Similarly, Green City, built for one million people, consisted
of a ribbon-like development of box-like houses, both sides exposed
to light and open spaces.[9] Productivity areas were set apart.[10]
Roads were planned for industry and agriculture, with the housing
alongside protected from dust and noise by a green belt. There
were laybys on the highways – in Magnitogorsk every kilometre

and in Green City every 500 metres. Various centres catered for different housing districts and included dining-rooms, sports facilities, libraries, rest rooms and hairdressers. In addition to this, in Magnitogorsk there were cultural centres, clubs and parks attractively situated on each road. The central administration lay between the main roads together with the Park of Culture and was the centre of all political and civic activities. Opposite this, surrounded by plantations, were schools for children and cultural activities for adults. Crèches lay closest to the housing estate, followed by kindergartens, then hostels for school children.

Both projects included houses assembled on the site from standard prefabricated materials. Silicate blocks were used mainly in Magnitogorsk and standard wooden frames, together with fibre-board, in Green City.[11]

Barshch, however, was not content. In an article written with Zyndblatov in 1933, he protested against a narrow, functional approach to housing, deploring the barrack-like appearance of those 'living boxes' and appealing for a new conception of architecture. He attached great importance to structures in their relationship to human requirements. For the next ten years, under

193

193 M. Barshch and M. Ginsburg: Guiprogor, a sector of the Baschkirsk works, housing in the Chernigov industrial area, prototype, 1932

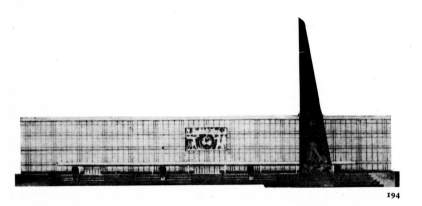

194

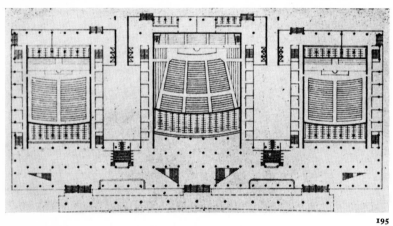

195

196

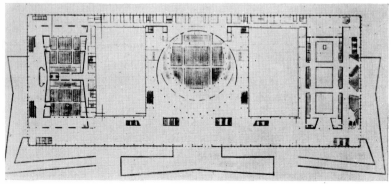

197

194, 195 M. Barshch, B. Datuk,
G. Krivuchenko with the collaboration of
V. Romanovsky: competition project for
the Palace of USSR Councils, 1957

196, 197 Alternative to the above project,
1959

Zholtokovsky, he organized various projects in Moscow (1933, 1945 and 1948) and in Minsk (1948, 1949), at the State Institute for Town Planning in 1950 and the Special Department of Architectural Construction from 1953 to 1960. He was most active during the crucial period of Soviet architecture from 1956 to 1959. He competed, with success, for the planning of cinemas, theatres and clubs in the experimental district for the reconstruction of Ivanov. The monument to Tsiolkovsky in Kaluga and an obelisk in Moscow are also his work. Nevertheless, he is most celebrated for his early work. In 1957, however, his project for the Palace of USSR Councils attracted the attention of the Architectural Society. His colleagues were Datuk, Krivuchenko, Romanovsky, Barkhin and Novikov. Its success led to the idea of changing the Palace into an all-union-forum. This was a reminder of the early years following the October Revolution, when a motion was carried for the construction of such a palace as a communal building for the USSR.

Barshch has been professor at the Moscow Institute of Architecture since 1935.

(translation Elizabeth Heath)

1 *Contemporary Architecture* no. 3, 1927, p. 81.
2 *Contemporary Architecture* no. 3, 1927, p. 81.
3 M. Ginsburg *Housing* Moscow 1934, p. 120.
4 M. Ginsburg *Housing* Moscow 1934, p. 138.
5 M. Ginsburg *Housing* Moscow 1934, p. 148.
6 M. Ginsburg *Housing* Moscow 1934, pp. 149–150.
7 M. Ginsburg *Housing* Moscow 1934, p. 148.
8 M. Ginsburg *Housing* Moscow 1934, pp. 148–149.
9 M. Ginsburg *Housing* Moscow 1934, p. 149.
10 M. Ginsburg *Housing* Moscow 1934, p. 151.
11 M. Ginsburg *Housing* Moscow 1934, p. 153.

The Golosov Brothers

V. V. Kyrilov

During the 1920s Soviet architecture was inseparably linked with the name Golosov; there were two Golosov brothers, Pantelemon and Ilya, both of whom are deserving of individual study.

Pantelemon Golosov (1882–1945) was one of the leading Constructivist architects. Remarkably gifted, he was also a fine painter and an excellent engineer. Although during his lifetime he was not as obviously successful as his brother Ilya, his contribution to architecture was of equal and perhaps even greater importance. His *Pravda* building in Moscow is one of the finest examples of Soviet architecture of the period.

198 Pantelemon Golosov

Born in Moscow in 1882, Golosov graduated from the Moscow College of Painting, Sculpture and Architecture in 1912. Though not a classicist, his work was imbued with a classic elegance, rhythm and proportion. Even before the Revolution he was anxious to establish a new architecture. He was, therefore, particularly interested in the 'modern' style and fascinated by the possibilities of using new materials such as reinforced concrete, glass and metal. He liked best the simplest of forms, as is evident in his design of 1913 for the Vargin house in Ulansky Street, Moscow.

199

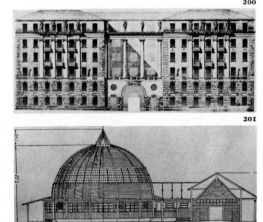

200

201

199 P. Golosov: the Vargin house, Ulansky Street, Moscow, 1913, design

200 P. and I. Golosov: the Gabrichesky house, Moscow, 1913, design

201 P. Golosov and Zholtovsky: pavilion Agricultural and Crafts Exhibition, Moscow, 1923

But the pre-Revolutionary period was scarcely suited to the development of experimental rationalism in architecture. After the Revolution he was able to experiment in the use of concrete, and was encouraged even by his classicist teachers, Zholtovsky and Shchusev. In the Mossoviet studios he worked on the general plan for Moscow, and designed a domed timber cattle-breeders' pavilion for the Agricultural and Crafts Exhibition. In 1923 he was particularly active, designing a Palace of Work for Moscow, a House of Assembly for Briansk, a House of the People for Novo-Vosnessensk, and a hospital for Samarkand.

He then turned to housing. He entered competitions for workers' housing estates at Simonovsk and Zamoskverechy, and at Ivano-Voznessensk. He also designed a garden city on a radial pattern, the whole carefully zoned.

This somewhat simplified rationalist approach had much in common with that of the members of OSA, inspired in particular by Ginsburg, and it was accordingly with that movement that he allied himself. Thereafter, taking a lead from Ginsburg, he concentrated even more fixedly on the problems of housing, and related social and communal buildings. But working with the members of OSA, he soon began to criticize their approach; he found their work dry and lacking in sensibility. He moved somewhat away from their simplified form of functionalism to find a richer form of expression in the design of workers' clubs. His railway workers' union of 1927 is one of the most interesting of his designs of this period. The elements are asymmetrically grouped around a stair well, which acts as a kind of pivot for a loose but highly convincing composition. He adopted a similar arrangement for the designs for the Lenin library (1928) and the Academy of Industry, Moscow (1928).

202, 203 P. Golosov: railway workers' union club, 1927, design

His fertiliser research institute, Moscow, was built between 1931 and 1933. He also built the post office in Kharkov in 1927 and Radio House in 1931.

In the late twenties Golosov had turned to industrial architecture. One of his most important executed works was the Kinofabrik in Moscow. Studios are strung along corridors, communication being easy and access independent. The administration building is in a vertical tower. Concrete, metal and glass are the prime materials.

His masterpiece was the *Pravda* building, built in 1934; it is a symbol of the new industrial Russia, and was intended as such.

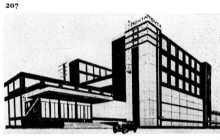

207

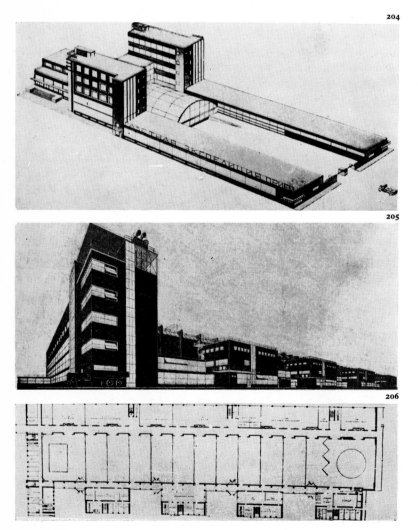

204

205

206

208

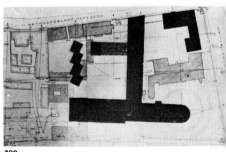

209

204, 207 P. Golosov: post office, Kharkov, 1927, design
205, 206 P. Golosov: Kinofabrik, Moscow, 1927; axonometric and plan
208, 209 P. Golosov: Lenin Library, Moscow, 1928, design

210

211

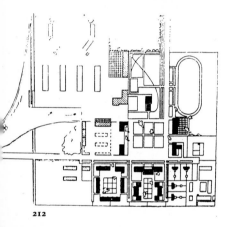

212

213

214

It is made of two units, a seven-storey editorial building (horizontally glazed) and a low printing works. The simple form of the editorial offices is enlivened by the contrast of blank walling and glazing and by the entrance portico. The interior is equally carefully composed, and most delicately lit. Certainly it is one of the most elegant of Constructivist buildings, rivalling even Le Corbusier's Central Union building.

At the same period Golosov prepared plans for a village community, the *sovkhoz* 'Zernotress', but it was not built.

Socialism was well established by the early 1930s, but the architecture that had been designed as its counterpart was not so readily accepted; it seemed dull and lifeless to most people. Above all, it lacked any sense of special popular character. Golosov was only too well aware of this.

Between 1930 and 1940 he concentrated on the rebuilding of Moscow and road works – in particular, the Kolujskoe Road. He and his team were also occupied with other important projects, such as the Alma-Ata and the Moscow Exhibition of 1939, the House of Councils in Vladivostock (1939), the Moscow hostel for artists on the Dragomilov Embankment (1939–1940), the *Izvestia* building (1940), the Ogiza building, etc. His work at this time was influenced by classical tradition. He used a variety of decorative elements disrupting rudely the early elegance of his architecture. His last work was a department store designed in 1940. Worn out by illness and the misfortunes of war, he died in 1945.

Besides being an outstanding architect, Golosov was an exceptional leader. For years he was in charge of workshop no. 9 at the Mossoviet and workshop no. 2 at the Narkomtyazhprom. He trained many architects such as Savitsky, Bekov, Rejov, Rosenfeldt and Uganov. As a professor at the Moscow Institute of Architecture, he devoted himself to the training of people destined to make a framework for the architecture of the future.

210, 211 P. Golosov: *Pravda* building, Moscow, 1930–34

212 P. Golosov: plan of the *sovkhoz* 'Zernotress'

213 P. Golosov: *Izvestia* buildings, Kievsky Square, Moscow, 1940, design for portion of the façade

214 P. Golosov: artist's hostel on the Dragomilov Embankment, Moscow 1940, façade to the court

Ilya Golosov (1883–1945) was educated together with his elder brother, Pantelemon, at the Stroganov College. Both became architects, Ilya graduating from the Moscow College of Painting, Sculpture and Architecture in 1912. At this point any similarity between the brothers ends. Their temperaments were completely different.

Ilya Golosov had a sensitive, emotional nature. He was primarily a painter, but also a brilliant engineer and architect. He started work before the Revolution – designing houses, churches and public buildings. He was initially influenced by classicism, and this was reflected in his early work – Zimeev's houses in Kirjace (1912), Zuev's houses in Moscow (1913) – his brother Pantelemon, also worked on this project. He experimented, in addition, with popular architecture (a wooden church at the Petrovsk Factory in 1916) and with other styles, but his work was disappointing. Modern art did not appeal to him, he preferred the classical masters. The Revolution, however, spurred him on to something new. He decided to concentrate on theory and teaching. At VKHUTEMAS and the Polytechnic, he lectured on the new concepts of architecture. New forms, he held, arise from new means of construction. But in order to understand true creativity, it is essential to find out the true laws of beauty. Such laws apply equally to the present and the past and the architect must therefore know, by rational analysis, how to blend the two. Golosov himself constantly studied historical architecture.

215 Ilya Golosov

He spent some time at the Mossoviet, learning from such older men as Shchusev and Zholtovsky. In this transition period his work already showed a certain richness and monumentality, later to become characteristic – the Moscow Exhibition of Agriculture and Crafts (1923), a pavilion of the Far East (1919), a crematorium (1918), the Basman Hospital in Moscow (1919), the Memorial School at Yashaya Polyana and the general plan for Moscow.

He attempted to modernize the classical style and did much experimental work, breaking away from strict academicism. He was captivated by the use of various geometric forms, shapes and surfaces – a radio station (1921), a Palace of Work in Moscow (1923). Upholding a functionalist approach, Golosov was of necessity a member of the OSA, yet he deplored their utilitarian attitudes. He was opposed to Ginsburg and most members of the group. Constructivism to Ilya was simply a means to solve technical problems.

By the end of the twenties, his style had crystallized and his

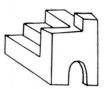
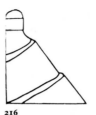

216

217

216 I. Golosov: experiment in form: period
of architectural symbolism

217, 218 I. Golosov: Palace of Work,
Moscow, 1923

219 I. Golosov: Palace of Work,
Rostov-on-Don, perspective

220 I. Golosov: House of Councils,
Briansk, 1924

221 I. Golosov: House of Councils,
Khabarovsk, 1929, design

218

219   **220**

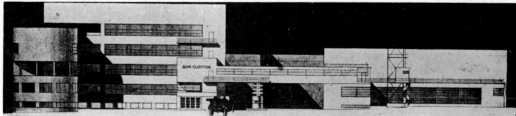

221

222

223

224

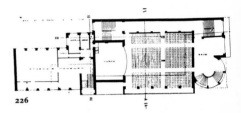

225

reputation had been established. He worked on public, cultural and administrative buildings (houses of council and administration in Briansk, 1924; Alma-Ata, 1925; Elist, 1927; Khabarovsk, 1929). His design for the Palace of Work, Rostov-on-Don (1930) is typical of his work of this period.

In Moscow, he built the Telegraph building (1926) and, in the same year, the Textile building, a huge construction, almost entirely of glass. His design for the Electrobank (1927) was similar. His Rusgertorg includes a cylindrical glass cage, enclosing a stairway, meeting a rectangular form on the top floor. This became a favourite device and appeared again in Golosov's greatest work, the club of the Professional Association of all Community Workers (Lesny Street, Moscow, 1926). The façade is a combination of glass and blank walls, conveying the idea of a gigantic machine – symbolic of industry and work.

His competition design for a Palace of Culture, Stalingrad, 1928, was much admired. It showed a new concern for sculptural effect; though the intersecting cylinder and rectangle served once again as the point of departure.

Golosov worked long on the design of a new, popular theatre, taking part in many competitions for such projects (Ivano-Voznessensk, 1930; Mossoviet, 1932; Meyerhold, 1932; MOSPS, 1934; and

226

222 I. Golosov: Textile building, Moscow, 1926, design
223 I. Golosov: Central Telegraph building, Moscow, 1926, design
224, 225 I. Golosov: Electrobank, Moscow, 1927, design
226–228 I. Golosov: workers' club on Lesny Street, Moscow, 1926

227 228

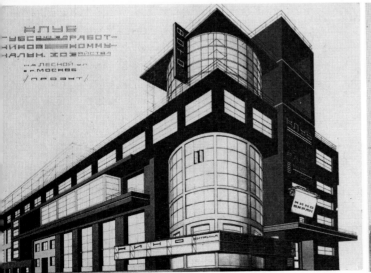

229

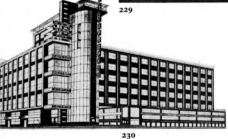

230

231

233

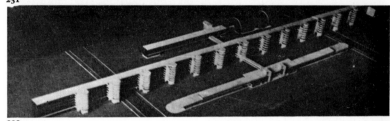

232

234

229 I. Golosov: Palace of Culture, Stalingrad, 1926

230 I. Golosov: Rusgertorg, Moscow, 1926, design

231 I. Golosov: theatre in Sverdlovsk, 1928, design

232 I. Golosov: community house in Stalingrad, 1928

233 I. Golosov: Novkombet, Moscow, 1928, design

234 I. Golosov: housing estate at Ivano-Voznessensk, 1931, design

in both Moscow and Minsk for the BSSR, 1934). The Sverdlovsk project of 1930 was his best. He conceived the idea that the public should perform. The stage could be entirely transformed and allowed to be used for demonstrations and military parades. But from then on Golosov's work became more and more influenced by classicism.

Public building did not prevent him from studying the problems of communal housing. He had already worked on the planning of houses and flats for workers in Ivano-Voznessensk (1926) and in Moscow (1924) and he turned the more readily to the development of communal dwelling units (a housing estate at Ivano-Voznessensk, 1931; a block of flats in Moscow, 1928) for the Novkombet. His planning remained functional – see, for ·instance, his designs for communal dwellings in Stalingrad (1928) – but 'artistry' was added in an artistic and dynamic way.

When Constructivism was condemned Golosov welcomed the reversion and lost no time in readapting the old formulae. There could be no creativity, he held, without an understanding of the true principles of classical architecture. He was now in direct conflict with OSA and his brother Pantelemon, a staunch supporter of Constructivism. The state competition for the Palace of Workers, organized in 1931, was intended to settle the raging controversy. Ilya Golosov's project was dominated by inspiration, and was overwhelmed with decorative elements. His style deteriorated, becoming increasingly monumental.

In the mid-thirties, Golosov turned once again to administrative buildings – the House of Books in Ogiza (1934), the Tass offices (1936), the supply and administration building (1939), the building for the Komintern executive (1939) and the Narkomstrol building in Progovsky Street, Moscow (1939). In 1934 he built workers' houses in the Yausky Boulevard, Moscow, and the hydro-electric station in Gorky (1936–40).

Before the war, Golosov was engaged in the development of old towns. In Moscow, he worked on the plan for the south-east district (1936), Tagansky Square (1939), Frunzensky Embankment (1939) and the first metro station (1934).

During the war he excelled at designing memorials. His last work was a project for the memorial museum to the Soviet Army. He died in 1945.

All his life, Golosov had been concerned with education. He ran workshop no. 4 at the Mossoviet. He was, for many years, professor at VKHUTEMAS, the Moscow Polytechnic and MAI.

235 I. Golosov: house for workers in the Yausky building, Moscow, 1934 (workers of the academy of military engineering)

'The architect Pantelemon Golosov' B.S.E. First ed. Vol. XVII, p. 486; Second ed. Vol. XI p. 633

P. Golosov 'I approach work with joy' *Building in Moscow*. No. 9, 1933.

P. Golosov and K. Rejov 'Our early works' *Building in Moscow*. No. 2, 1934.

E. Kornfield *Golosov and the Pravda Building*.

A. Levin 'The architect Pantelemon Golosov' *Architecture of the USSR*. No. 2, 1968.

I. Golosov 'My path of creativity' *Architecture of the USSR*. No. 1, 1933.

R. Khiger 'The architect Ilya Golosov (review of his work)' *Architecture of the USSR*. No. 1, 1933.

'The architect Ilya Golosov' B.S.E. 1st ed. Vol. XVII, p. 486.

'The architect Ilya Golosov' B.S.E. 2nd ed. Vol. XI, p. 633.

The architect I. Golosov' *Catalogue of exhibited works*, Moscow 1946.

I. Golosov 'New paths in architecture' Lectures at MAO. From *History of Soviet Architecture*, Materials and Documentation published by A.N.S.S.R., Moscow, 1963.

(translation Elizabeth Heath)

A. Burov 1900-57

V. Khazanova

236 Andrei Burov

Andrei Burov's work is full of surprises. In his presentation drawings there are no elevations with landscaped backgrounds, no conventional figures, no romantic skies. Although he was a master at handling both pencil and brush, architectural design was never for him an end in itself.

Not all his projects were worked out or even thought out with equal thoroughness, but every one of them has a basic idea, which often became the starting point for further research, not only for his adherents, but even for his opponents, while Burov himself, with an inventor's passion, was already concentrating on something new.

It is not wise to indulge in conjectures about Burov's architectural outlook. Skilled in polemics, a good orator who knew how to captivate large numbers of listeners, a gifted writer, he himself described in a series of widely read articles published in architectural journals between 1933 and 1956, all that had stirred him during the last twenty-five years of his life. His brilliant book, *About Architecture*, written during 1943–44 and published in 1960 after the author's death, summarizes his ideas.

Long before the book appeared, its basic principles had been stated by the author in various articles, which were popular among architects. Moreover, the appeal of Burov's book was not confined to specialists. Members of the most varied professions were fascinated by it. It may even be considered a more lasting memorial to its author than the buildings he designed.

The book is meditative: it speculates about life and the place occupied in it by architecture; it touches upon all the most difficult questions of the period. But Burov was unable to find solutions for a number of the problems by which he was himself disturbed. Moreover, divergences occurred between his concept of architecture and its realization in his works.

Burov was born in 1900, the son of an architect. From 1918 to 1925 he studied at VKHUTEMAS. While still a student he successfully took part in the famous architectural competition assigning projects for the Moscow Agricultural and Craft Exhibition (1923) and, at

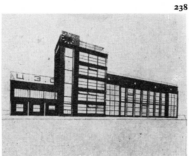

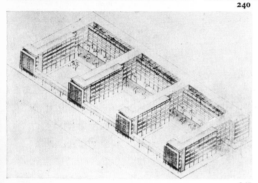

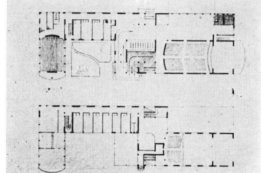

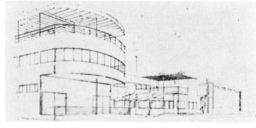

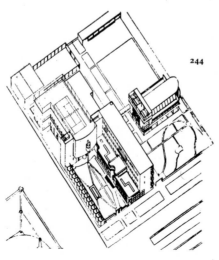

237 A. Burov: Moscow central railway station, diploma project VKHUTEMAS. A. Vesnin's studio, 1925

238 A. Burov: central power plant, Kiev, 1927, project

239 A. Burov and M. Parusnikov: workmen's dwellings in Ivanovo-Voznessensk, 1926, competition project

240 A. Burov, M. Sinyavsky and M. Barshch: House of Industry in Sverdlovsk, 1927

242, 243 A. Burov: club for 500 members, 1927

241, 244 A. Burov: union club for workers in the food industry in Moscow, 1928, project

246

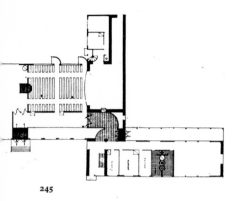

245

about the same time, he also started teaching. During that period he was a member of the LEF group (1922–24).

In 1925 he completed his studies at VKHUTEMAS in A. Vesnin's studio. His diploma thesis – a project for a central railway station in Moscow – received immediate approval and he was given the highest award for graduates, namely, a trip abroad.

Burov started his career as a convinced Functionalist-Constructivist. He was one of the founder members of the Union of Contemporary Architects, which was established in Moscow in December 1928, and a member of the first publishing board of the Union's journal, *Contemporary Architecture*.

After receiving his diploma in 1927, he incorporated the new principles of Constructivism into projects for workers' dwellings and clubs. He received a number of prizes and was able to carry out some of his plans; his name often appeared in architectural journals. He was the set designer for Serge Eisenstein's *The General Line*, and, while working on the film, was intrigued by the idea that he was, in a sense, modelling the future. In the unpublished article 'Architecture and the Cinema' he wrote:

'The cinema opens out possibilities for the architect and, in fact for all of us, to accomplish things impossible to realize hitherto for a number of reasons. The architect works in the cinema not as a decorator, but as an architect. . . . I aimed to produce not merely decorative effects but, by means of the film, to introduce new methods of industrialized architecture and to design buildings built with new materials and by modern methods. . . . In the same way, had the cinema presented me with the problem of designing a workman's dwelling, a public building or even a whole town (Dziga Vertov once discussed the possibilities of involving me in that type of work for the film *Forward, Soviet*), I would have accepted the challenge and shown that the problem could be solved . . . as one of the creators of the awareness and forms of a new way of life . . . dwellings . . . should form a complex of elements indissolubly tied together. . . . I see [in the cinema] above all an excellent means of spreading among the

245, 246 A. Burov: club for workers in the food industry in Tver, 380 members, 1928

masses the great ideas of our time. . . . The cinema should . . .
show what is, as well as what ought to be . . .'[1]

In the Central State Archives of Literature and Art, where this
article is kept, there are several photographs showing him with two
other men. One of them appears slightly supercilious, rather tense.
The other two, wearing almost identical leather coats, look
detached. This trio is Le Corbusier, Eisenstein and Burov. The
photographs were taken in November 1928, when Le Corbusier
visited Moscow where the Central Union building was being built.
Le Corbusier was shown fragments of the still unfinished film
General Line. This is what Eisenstein said about it at the time:

'[General Line] . . . was of special interest to him [Le Corbusier]
in as far as part of it consisted of propaganda of the particular
type of architecture, 'machines for living in' (as Le Corbusier
calls them), which he was creating. It showed a *sovkhoz* [state
farm], specially built for *General Line* by A. Burov, one of the
most devoted followers of Le Corbusier. Le Corbusier was
delighted by Burov's *sovkhoz* and admitted that he was very
much surprised to find in Russia an application of identical
architectural principles and forms, which yet produced a quite
different result from those in the West . . .'[2]

Five years later, in 1933, Burov wrote about this period:

'I moved away from Constructivism in 1927–8 . . . Constructivism presented the problem correctly at a time when we had to
get rid of accumulated concepts in architecture. . . . It seemed
right, then, to have functional buildings as a basis, but, as work
proceeded, it became clear that such buildings alone were not
enough. . . .'[3]

A decade later, Burov made a further analysis of Constructivism
and explained his and many others' 'dissatisfaction with this
movement which, in the twenties had seemed capable of performing
a miracle in architecture'. His verdict on Constructivism is severe:

'From the point of view of handling material, Constructivism
was nothing but archaism. . . . Material and structure prevailed
over form. The style was Baroque (without the ornamentation),
for the project was planned in an imaginary material (reinforced concrete is not brick). There was a strong Muslim

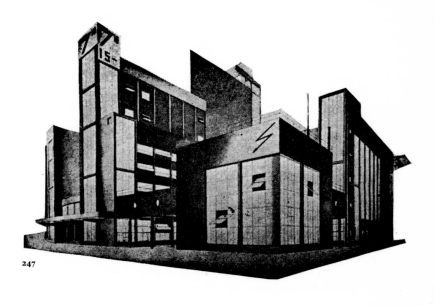

247

247 A. Burov: theatre project, 1924

influence and orthodox Mahommedanism at that; by way of
decoration only clocks and letters were allowed.'[4]

These words of Burov's are best illustrated by his own project for
a theatre (1924), in which, with the wholehearted enthusiasm of a
neophyte, he embodied all the edicts of Constructivism of the
1920s.

Burov was, however, sincere when writing these words; by
1927–8 he was genuinely disappointed in Constructivism. Together
with many of his colleagues, he was painfully striving to discover
new ways in architecture. The search for the new led him to study
the classical heritage. However, for Burov – the theorist – turning
to classicism never implied imitation. In 1934 he wrote that:

'in practice, one often finds that, while assimilating a cultural
inheritance . . . one assimilates the false procedures of an
illusory architecture and tries to achieve an illusion of antiquity
with contemporary materials'.[5]

Yet, at the time when he wrote this, Burov – the practising architect – was responsible for a building in Gorky Street, Moscow,
which ten years later he himself placed in the category of 'academic
sculptural–architectural designs'.[6] This self criticism was by no
means a tardy act of repentance. Burov recognized the correctness
of a direct approach to classicism suggesting a new method – a

deliberate theatricalization, which he never related to the 'general
way of the future development of architecture', but considered
suitable for 'isolated cases' only.[7]

Theatrical classicism preferred the possibility of establishing
contact between history and modern times. It was along those lines
that Burov and A. Vlassov devised the project of the Meyerhold
theatre in 1933 – straightforward theatrical decorations on the
walls of the theatre-building itself. This was followed by the
stylized design of the nine halls of the State Historical Museum in
Moscow (1937). Finally – the end of the search – the architect's
house in Moscow (1940) forms a paraphrase of Piero della
Francesca's fresco *The Finding of the True Cross* in San Francesco
at Arezzo.

Ancient Rome, Pompeii, Russia in the days of Ivan the Terrible,
Peter the Great, Elisabeth, the Italian Renaissance, all as seen by a
man of the thirties, set the tone for Burov's projects and constructions. He considered that, sometimes:

248

249

> 'a single structure can be subordinate to the character of the
> whole or to the symbolic traditional form inherent in a given
> structure; in such cases, form should not be disguised by the
> 'academic' method, but should be theatricalized. . . .'[8]

The 'theatricalization of classicism' is but one, and a very rare
method of assimilating the inheritance. It would be wrong to think
that Burov confined himself to it. His enthusiasm for classicism
was transient, whereas the study of the principles of the development of universal and national architecture consumed him. Revising,
years later, the theory and practice of Functionalism-Construc-
tivism, Burov did not refute a single one of its main postulates,
which stated that the national aspect of architecture is determined
by centuries-old living and climatic conditions, by demands of the
new social order and the advance of modern techniques.

250

Burov became interested in the popular architecture of the south
of Russia as early as 1927, when he was designing trade union
clubs for the southern regions. In November 1938 he completed
one of his most successful projects – 'a typical dwelling for a
kolkhoz [collective] in southern Crimea'. It was based on the popular
dwellings that had been built in the south for centuries.

Burov considered that 'architecture cannot originate from
science or technique alone, only from expediency . . .'[9] The whole
of his work is permeated by the urge to combine art with science.
He was convinced that:

248 A. Burov: dwelling house, 25 Gorki
Street, Moscow, two phases of construction
1935–50

249 A. Burov and A. Vlassov: project for
theatre in Mayakovsky Place, 1934

250 A. Burov: own residence, Moscow, 1940

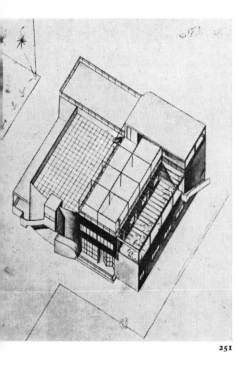

251

251 A. Burov: project for a club for workers in the food industry in the extreme south of the USSR

'architecture ought to be human, linked with nature, descriptive, plastic, tectonic and contemporary ... New plastic art is sculptural and polychromatic, it should take its origins from our surroundings, from nature and from the mighty traditions of popular art. That is where our roots are.'[10]

However, there was no direct way to create such an architecture. This is felt particularly in the work of Burov himself, where one finds both creative successes and compromises. For instance, both the project for Univermag on Kosmomol Square (1936) and the one for Moscow airport (1939) show a fear of the smoothness of bare walls, not a Burov characteristic, which he disguised by designing a building unsuitable for the particular scale required and by naïve symbolism. Moreover, the two projects he completed before the war for a building to house the panorama *Storming of Perekop*, he himself described as follows:

'I believe these were two of my least successful designs. I could not imagine what kind of design was needed for a building which had to be treated as a memorial.'[11]

In spite of that, Burov occupies a special place as one of the founders of prefabricated dwelling systems. As far back as 1934, he remarked:

'Mass production cannot be given just any old form; it is subordinated to the specific methods of production. For instance, the material and methods of production of a standard article should be in harmony. Given the correct approach, a standard article can and should be an object of art.'[12]

Starting from these premises, Burov and the architect B. Blokhin designed and built precast buildings in Moscow in 1939–40. Burov maintained that:

'it was possible to build a house from identical elements, not only because this is the outcome of prefabrication, but also because the contents of the house are identical ... flats ... rooms ...'[13]

Burov and Blokhin tried to find an expressive method of construction, corresponding to the large-scale elements. However the heavy, inert mass of the walls did not relate to the lighter nature of the enclosing window walls. They tried to overcome this heaviness in their next building and decided to mask the visual effect of precast blocks, covering them with rustic masonry. The walls lost their heaviness, but also their expressiveness. After that, Burov gave up the decorative application of imitation stone. In the last of his prefabricated apartments which he himself considered to be significant, the large units are again clearly visible. They are, however, no longer in monotonous layers, but in a particular order, with a clear distinction between non-load-bearing units and supporting walls, columns, etc. – like the columns and architraves of classical architecture.

Burov was endowed with foresight. In the years when, for the sake of ill-conceived monumentality, there was a tendency to turn every dwelling into a florid memorial of the 'period', he was trying to develop the construction technique of genuine mass-dwellings. 'Town-dwelling is one of the principal links in the economy of the State', he wrote. 'Let us create memorials for history and dwellings for our contemporaries.'[14] He tried to incorporate these ideas into a building on the Leningrad Prospekt in Moscow.

Burov was particularly taken with the idea of lessening the strains of a modern, many-storey town and of eliminating them altogether in the future. In a project for the modernization of the seaside resort of Yalta (1944–5), he subordinated the skyscraper and the car to the convenience of the inhabitants. The embankment, entirely freed from traffic, became a seaside promenade. Part of the road was to run under the embankment with enormous openings overlooking the sea on one side of the tunnel. Carefully preserving the vegetation in the old, low-level part of the town, he scattered in it multi-storey buildings, supported by light arcades.

The advance of science, coupled with his own ability to dream and to foresee, led Burov to seriously consider the possibility of creating an artificial micro-climate in towns and dwellings of the Arctic. A few decades later this idea was to become an actuality.

'What is architecture?' Burov asks in his book, and he answers, 'Architecture is the environment in which humanity has its existence, which opposes nature and connects man with nature, an environment which humanity creates in order to exist and which it leaves as a legacy to its heirs.'[15] His whole life was a search for the lost wholeness of architecture, a search in the name of humanity. The Parthenon aroused in him 'a sense of pride in humanity'. The ruins of the Roman temples at Baalbek appeared to him 'monstrous in their enormity and majesty'. He felt that they had ceased to be architecture, representing instead 'tyranny incarnate in stone'

252

253

254

252 A. Burov and B. Blokhin: dwelling house of prefabricated units on the Big Polianka, 1939–40

253, 254 A. Burov and B. Blokhin: dwelling house built of large units, 25 Leningrad Prospekt, Moscow, 1940–41

255 A. Burov (collaborators – S. Vassin, D. Metaniev): project for dwelling house – SVAM section (fibreglass) 1956

and that 'under these stones, under their weight and their inordinate dimensions, architecture has been lost to man.'[16]

At one time he forsook architecture to study physics at the Physical Institute of the Academy of Sciences, where he received an honorary doctor's degree and published a number of significant scientific articles.

(translation Marina Corby)

1 Central State Archives of Literature and Art of the USSR (TSGALI USSR) f. 1928, op. I, d. 21, pp. 1–2.
2 TSGALI USSR f. 1923, op. I, d. 978, pp. 1–6.
3 *USSR Architecture* nos. 3–4, 1933, p. 18.
4 A. Burov *About Architecture* p. 26.
5 *USSR Architecture* no. 4, 1934, p. 36.
6 A. Burov *About Architecture* p. 51.
7 A. Burov *About Architecture* p. 51.
8 Burov *ibid* p. 52.
9 Burov *ibid* p. 94.
10 Burov *ibid* p. 136.
11 Burov *ibid* p. 90.
12 *USSR Architecture* no. 4, 1934, p. 36.
13 A. Burov *About Architecture* p. 97.
14 A. Burov *ibid* pp. 55–56.
15 A. Burov *ibid* p. 145.
16 A. Burov *ibid* p. 119.

I. I. Leonidov 1902-1959

S. O. Khan-Mahomedov

Ivan Ilich Leonidov was a pioneer of new forms: during his short but brilliant career he produced designs that were to become paradigms for the whole of the modern movement in architecture.

Most of his childhood was spent in the country, where he sometimes worked as an apprentice to the village icon painter, and at other times travelled to Petrograd to work. In 1920, he joined the newly organized 'free artists' studios' in Tver; he was taught drawing and painting there and the following year was sent to Moscow to continue his studies at VKHUTEMAS. Later he moved to the faculty of architecture where he joined a group under the supervision of Aleksandr Vesnin, who was to have a great influence on him.

But Leonidov was an original. From 1925 onwards he entered architectural competitions and won several prizes – 'An improved peasant cottage' (1925), 'Minsk university', 'Prototype workers' clubs for 500 and 1,000' (1926). He joined the Constructivist movement, OSA, while still studying, and later became a member of the editorial board of its journal *Contemporary Architecture*. His diploma design, 'A printing house for *Izvestia*, Moscow' (1926) was a typical Constructivist project.

At the time Constructivism was in danger of degenerating into a mere stylistic application. But Leonidov gave to it a new coherence and in particular a new understanding of form and composition, best illustrated by his final-year project for the Lenin Institute, Moscow, 1927. This consisted of two principal forms: a vast auditorium – something of an innovation in itself – in the form of a sphere, glazed on the top half with seating in the lower half, and, adjacent to it, the library, designed as a slender vertical element. The relationship of the two is a most important feature of the composition and this spatial dynamism was extended over the whole site in the arrangement of subordinate elements along three definite axes. This way of making more vital and unifying subsidiary spaces by the use of interlocking axes was exploited more than once by Leonidov. The real impact, however, of his design derives from the extraordinary simplicity of his main forms – particularly

256 Ivan Ilich Leonidov

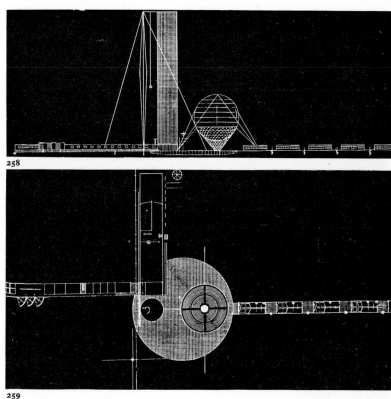

257–260 I. Leonidov: design for the Lenin Institute, 1927, two views of the model, elevation and plan

striking since most other architects were seeking expression in complexity. In addition, he used the latest structural techniques in a most direct and dramatic way.

His project was much approved at VKHUTEMAS; he was made an associate at once, and in 1928, at the students' request, appointed a lecturer.

Leonidov's most active years were from 1927 to 1930. He was a diligent and lively member of OSA; he talked at all gatherings. But he also worked hard on a series of competition designs, a film studio for Moscow, the Columbus memorial in Santa Domingo, an office building for the Ministry of Industry, Moscow, a communal settlement in Magnitogorsk and a government office in Alma-Ata.

In 1929, at the first OSA congress, he read a paper on workers' clubs and presented a design of his own. The elements were broken down into separate forms and set within a large park

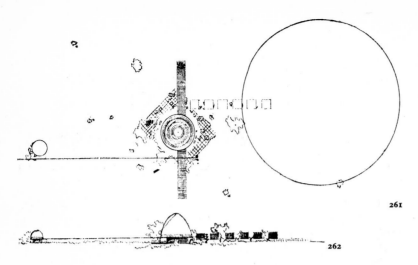

261

262

measuring 2400 square metres. The club was unusual in the range of buildings included – a conservatory, an auditorium, a library, a laboratory, sports halls, playing fields, a stadium and pavilions. The auditorium, covered by a parabolic vault, provided the main focus.

His design for a film studio incorporated an unusual variety of volumes and shapes, intended as film backgrounds, giving to it a complexity and picturesque appearance rarely found in his work – reminiscent of Malevich's compositions, which he greatly admired.

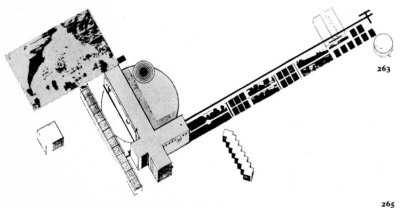

263

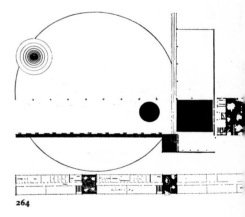

264

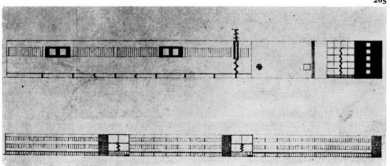

265

261, 262 I. Leonidov: variants A and B for workers' clubs, of a new social type, 1928

263–265 I. Leonidov: design for a film studio, Moscow, 1928

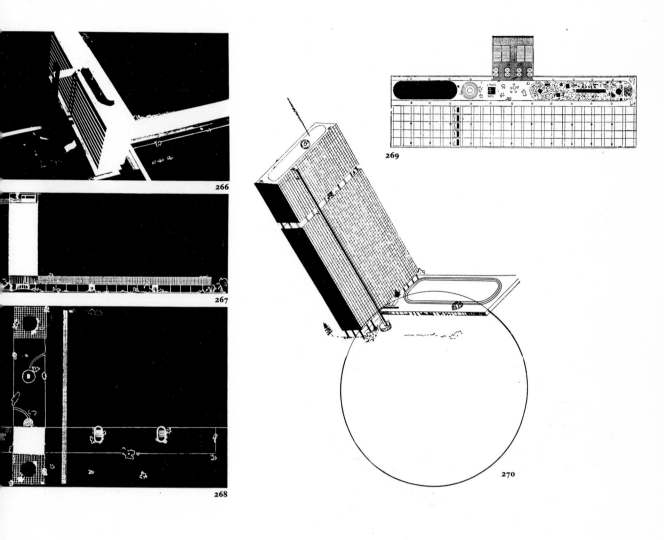

266

267

268

269

270

In the international competition for a Columbus memorial he rejected the programme for a monument, choosing rather to design a world cultural centre. He proposed an institute of interplanetary exploration, an observatory, a congress hall, a radio and television centre, an airport, etc. At the centre was a museum to Columbus, covered in glass, with air jets in place of walls.

Leonidov's designs for the House of Industry and the Central Union were among the first for rectangular office buildings with blank end walls and curtain walling in between.

266–268 I. Leonidov: design for the *Centrosoyuz* (Co-operative headquarters), Moscow, 1928; the competition was won by Le Corbusier, whose design was executed, in part, under the direction of N. Kolli

269, 270 I. Leonidov: design for an office building for the Ministry of Industry, Moscow, 1929–30

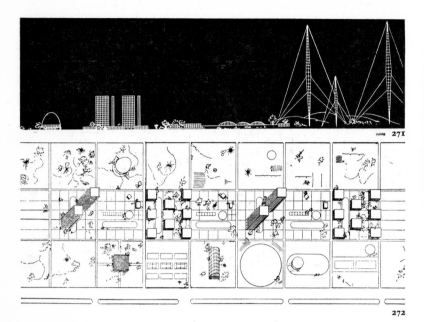

271

272

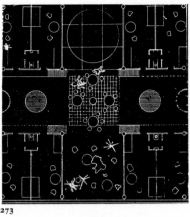

273

274

275

The Magnitogorsk project shows Leonidov as a town planner. He wanted no corridor streets, no buildings pushed to the street frontages and no courts. The town was to be developed in parallel lines of houses, running along main roads, with public buildings between. The industrial zone was to be at one extremity, the town extending from it into a green belt.

Leonidov's most important project was that for a Palace of Culture. As before, he departed from the conditions of the competition, proposing instead a cultural complex, an oasis within a residential district.

The site was divided into four areas to provide for mass demonstrations, physical culture, a sports stadium and science and research activities. Each area had distinctive buildings – the pyramidal sports hall, with a swimming bath surrounding it, for instance, and large glass-domed hall which could be divided with movable partitions. This design was vigorously attacked by members of VOPRA, who rejected such experimentation. At the end of 1930 they instigated a discussion of Leonidov's work, rejecting it as formalist and setting a dangerous precedent. They wanted no more such idealistic projects.

During 1930 Leonidov was busy on various schemes. He prepared drawings for the town of Igorky, he designed a square at the Serpukhovski Gate, Moscow, general plans for Moscow, the layout of the Hermitage gardens and a club for *Pravda*. All these designs are interesting, but they lack the earlier dynamism. Only

271–275 I. Leonidov: designs for the layout and detailed development of Magnitogorsk, 1930

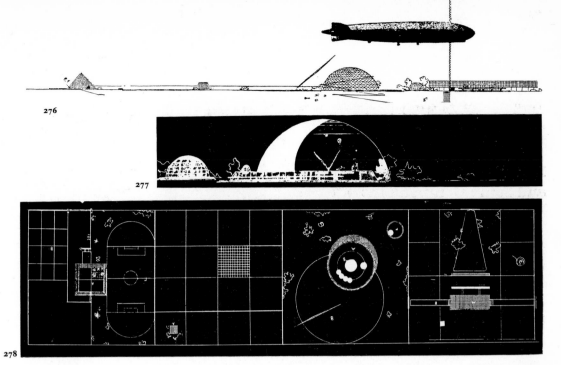

276

277

278

279

280

276–278 I. Leonidov: competition design for a Palace of Culture, Moscow, 1930

279 I. Leonidov: design for a house of heavy industry, on the side of the old Simonov monastery, Moscow, 1933

280 I. Leonidov's only executed work, a small amphitheatre, designed as part of a large scheme, under the direction of Ginsburg, at the Ordjonikidze sanatorium, at Kislovodsk in the Crimea, 1937

one late project, the House of Heavy Industry, in Red Square, Moscow, attains to the early mastery. The three glass towers are intricate and varied, deliberately related both formally and structurally to the towers of St Basil's and Ivan the Great's belfry.

During the late 1930s he designed the 'Kliuchiki' housing area near the Lower Taguil, the pioneer settlement 'Artek', another called 'Usul' in the Urals and a series of interiors. He actually built an amphitheatre and staircase in the gardens of one of the sanatoria in Kislovodsk.

After the war he turned to exhibition design – architectural design being thenceforth only a private hobby, but it included such projects as 'The towns of the sun' and a sketch for the UN building, New York.

Leonidov was a poet of pure form. He used the simplest of geometric volumes – cubes, rectangles, spheres, cylinders, cones and pyramids. He set them together with the utmost of sensibility. But the impact of his designs cannot be separated from his method of presentation. His drawing was extremely elegant. He would use white lines or gouache on natural wood or cardboard, employing both the softest and the most strident colours, and even gold. But the special interest of his work resides in the way in which he focused not on the forms, the buildings proposed, but the spaces between them. The airships, aeroplanes and aerials scattered throughout his projects are not just up-to-the-minute emblems, they are means of subtending space in another but altogether consistent way.

(translation Elizabeth Heath)

Appendices

List of Certain Executed Works and Some Competitions

1922   V. G. Shukhov (engineer): Radio tower, Moscow

1922–3   Competition for Palace of Labour, Moscow – projects by A. A. and L. A. Vesnin, Ginsburg, I. Golosov

1923   All-Russia Agricultural Exhibition, Moscow – pavilions by I. V. Zholtovsky, restaurant by V. A. Shchuko, and certain decorations by A. A. Ekster

1924   K. S. Melnikov: Sukharevka market, Moscow

1925   Paris Exhibition of Applied and Decorative Arts – Soviet Pavilion by Melnikov, includes work by, among others, Rodchenko, Lissitzky, Popova and Stepanova

1925–6   Competition for House of Textiles, Moscow – projects by Ginsburg, I. Golosov

1926   Vesnin brothers: Mostorg store

1926   I. Golosov: Workers' club, Lesny Street, Moscow

1927   K. Melnikov: Kauchuk workers' club, Moscow

1927   G. B. Barkhin: *Izvestia* building, Moscow

1927   V. Vesnin, N. Kolli, G. Orlov, S. Andriyevsky – Dneprogesa power station for the Dneiper Dam

1927–8   Competition for the Lenin library, Moscow – projects by Leonidov, P. Golosov and Vesnin brothers

1928   Competition for Centrosoyuz (Central Union building) Moscow – project by Leonidov, won by Le Corbusier

1928   A. S. Fufaev: Co-operative dwelling, Dukstraya, Moscow

1928–9   M. Ya. Ginsburg: Housing, Novinsky Boulevard, Moscow

1928–9   K. S. Melnikov: Rusakov club, Moscow

1929   K. S. Melnikov: Own residence, Moscow

1929   Barshch and Sinyavsky: Moscow planetarium

1929   Serafimov, Kravets, Fleger: House of State Industry (Gosprom), Dzerzhinsky Square, Kharkov.

1929–32   Competition for Palace of Soviets, Moscow – projects by Fomin, Ladovsky, Iofan *et al.*

281 I. A. Fomin: design for the Palace of the Soviets, Moscow, 1929

282

1930	I. S. Nikolaev: House-commune for students, Moscow
1930	Shchusev: Lenin mausoleum, Moscow
1930–5	P. Golosov: Pravda building, Moscow
1931	Vesnin brothers: ZIL Palace of Culture, Moscow
1931	Vesnin brothers: Project for state theatre, Kharkov
1933	A. A. and L. A. Vesnin: Savoda Lichanyeva Club, Moscow

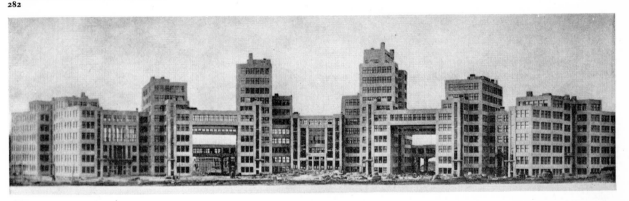

283

282 A Shchusev: Lenin's mausoleum, Moscow, 1930

283, 284 Serafimov, Kravets, Fleger: House of State Industry (Gosprom), Dzerzhinsky Square, Kharkov

284

List of Soviet architectural associations and their activities

V. Khazanova

MAO 1922–32

(Moscow Association of Architects) Re-established in 1922.
Former president Shekhtel. Vice-presidents S. Barkhov and P. Tolstev
Presidents: A. Shchusev, L. Vesnin
Vice-presidents: I. Rylsky, D. Makarov
Secretaries: P. Antipov, D. Rasov
Publications
Architecture, 1923, nos. 1–5
Editor: M. Ginsburg, assisted by L. Vesnin and E. Norbert
Special edition for the MAO competitions 1923–6 (1926)
Annuals of the MAO, nos. 5 and 6 (continuation of pre-Revolution-ary publication, 1928–30)
Editor: G. Barkhin
Editorial committee: P. Antipov, G. Barkhin, L. Vesnin, G. Goltz, N. Kolli, N. Markovnikov, I. Rylsky

LOA 1922–32

(Leningrad Association of Architects)
Founder members: V. Evald, G. Kosmachevsky, V. Karpovitch, N. Aistov, A. Tryasova, D. Mozalsky, G. Samusev, E. Rokitsky, V. Pavlovsky, N. Proskurnin, L. Ilyin, A. Nikolsky, F. Berenshtam, N. Katsenelenbogen, L. Borodulina, R. Kitner, S. Stepanov, A. Ol', N. Sakelev
President: V. Evald
Vice-president: G. Kosmachevsky
Secretary: E. Rokitsky
Treasurer: V. Pavlovsky
Librarian: A. Rosenberg
Editorial: L. Ilyin, V. Pokrovsky, M. Chizhov, F. Berenshtam, A. Kurilko, N. Aistov
Publications
The Architect – only one number in 1924
Editors: V. Karpovich, M. Khadzhi-Kasumov
Collaborators: L. Ilyin, P. Kosmachevsky, N. Proskurnin, A. Rosenberg, V. Rotkevitch, G. Samusev

OAKh

(Leningrad Association of Architects and Painters)
Presidents: L. Benoit, V. Rozhnovsky, V. Lesman
Vice-president: A. Grubbe
Secretaries: S. Nekrasov, N. Gundobin, I. Tkachenko
Publications
The Annual – restarted publication 1928 with no. 12
Editorial: A. Belogrud, V. Boloshinov, A. Dmitriev, I. Langard,
S. Nekrassov, B. Nikolaev, O. Muntz, S. Ovssanikov, L. Rudnev,
S. Serafimov, M. Sinyaver, V. Tvelkmeyer, N. Trotsky
Secretaries: N. Lanceret, M. Sinyaver
No. 14, covering the period 1930–33, came out in 1935. The
association was disbanded in 1932
Editorial: A. Belokrug, B. Boloshinov, N. Gundobin, A. Dmitriev,
E. Levinson, I. Langard, O. Muntz, S. Nekrassov, S. Ovssanikov,
V. Rozhnovsky, M. Sinyaver, A. Sokolov, I. Tkachenko, V. Tvelk-
meyer
General secretary: M. Sinyaver
The OAKh worked for a short time in Kiev. A project competition
was organized in 1923 for a House of the People in Sviatoshiny.
A professional association was organized in Moscow in 1918 with a
temporary Collective consisting of: M. Krokov, N. Strudkov,
Y. Reich, N. Baklanov, V. Voeikov, Y. Guerschten, Y. Dietrichs,
A. Ivanitsky, K. Keller, L. Kravetsky, A. Minor, A. Shchusev,
S. Belyabin, M. Ivanov, Kozlov and Ryazanov

ASNOVA 1923–32

(New Association of Architects)
Formed in Moscow in 1923. Incorporated into MOVANO in 1932
Founder members: N. A. Ladovsky, N. Dokuchaev, V. Krinsky,
A. Rukhlyadev, A. Efimov, V. Fidman, I. Mochalov, V. Balikhin
President and administrator: N. Ladovsky
President: M. Korzhev (1928–32)
Secretary: T. Varentsov
Publication
One number of *Asnova News*
Editors: El Lissitzky and N. Ladovsky

ARU Moscow 1928–32

(Association of Urban Architects)
Founder members: N. Ladovsky, D. Fridman, A. Zazersky,
V. Lavrov, G. Glushchenko, A. Grinberg, Dr Y. Nekrasov,

Dr Kovalev, G. Krutikov, S. Lopatin, the engineers A. Saishnikov
and B. Sakulin, the economist A. Zhirmunsky
President: N. Ladovsky
Vice-presidents: D. Fridman, A. Zazersky, V. Lavrov
Secretary: Y. Nekrasov
Leningrad section of ARU: A. Barutchev, I. Gilter, I. Meyerzon

OSA Moscow 1925–30
(Association of Contemporary Architects)
Incorporated into VANO in 1930, becomes SASS/VANO in 1931
Founder members: A. Vesnin, M. Ginsburg, Y. Kornfeld, V.
Vladimirov, A. Burov, G. Orlov, A. Kapustina, A. Fufaev, V.
Krassilnikov
President: A. Vesnin
Vice-presidents: M. Ginsburg and V. Vesnin
Secretary: G. Orlov
1926 associated to the State Academy of Fine Arts – GAHN
Publications
1926 *Contemporary Architecture* – six numbers each year
Editors: A. Vesnin and M. Ginsburg
No. 2 in 1929: M. Ginsburg
In 1930: R. Khiger
Secretary: N. Sokolov
Collaborators to the first editorials: A. Burov, A. Vesnin, V.
Vesnin, G. Bergman, V. Vladimirov, M. Ginsburg, I. Golosov, A.
Gan, A. Lolleit, I. Sobolev
Other collaborators:
1926: I. Matsa
1927: A. Pasternak and A. Nikolsky
1928: M. Barshch, N. Krasilnikov, Le Corbusier (Paris), I.
Leonidov, I. Muraviev, N. Sokolov, M. Kholostenko, F. Yalovkin,
A. Fisenko, P. Novitsky
1929: I. Nikolaev
1930: L. Komarova
25 April 1928 first conference
M. Ginsburg reports on 'Constructivism and architecture'
A. Nikolsky reports on 'New schools of construction'
Local accounts were sent in from all over Russia to headquarters
1929 first congress of OSA
Programme: housing and towns, communal building, technology
and science in architecture, materials, constructions, colour and
light, socialist communal problems, actual position of OSA within

contemporary architecture
Exhibition and displays during the congress
I. Leonidov reported on the building of clubs for workers
R. Khiger reported on formalism and the decadence of ideology in Soviet architecture
1930 OSA is incorporated into VANO
1931 it becomes the SASS/VANO
President: A. Nikolsky
Other members: I. Beldovsky, V. Galperrin, A. Krestin
In Kazan, supporters of the OSA form the OMA (Association of Young Architects)
Members: A. Gustov, Y. Kosyrev, V. Sotonin, I. Spiridonov, A. Trofimov, F. Yalovkin
Other branches in Baku, Tomsk, Kharkov, Kiev, Odessa, Sverdlovsk, Novossibirsk. They worked in various teaching establishments

OCTOBER Moscow 1929
(The All-State Workers' Association in the New Fields of Fine Art)
Founder Members: A. Alekseyev, A. Vesnin, V. Vesnin, E. Bais, A. Gan, M. Ginsburg, E. Gutnov, A. Damsky, A. Deineka, Dobrovsky, V. Elkin, L. Irbit, G. Klutsis, A. Kreichik, N. Lapin, I. Matsa, A. Mikhailov, D. Moor, P. Novitsky, A. Ostretsov, Diego Rivera, N. Sedelnikov, S. Senkin, Spirov, N. Talaksev, S. Telingater, B. Toot, B. Uits, P. Freiberg, E. Shub, N. Schneider, S. Eisenstein
This group worked together with the OSA, VOPRA, and VKHUTEIN
1931 Declaration for the fight for the proletarian positions in art. Meetings were held every two years

VOPRA Moscow 1929–32
(All-Russia Association of Proletarian Architects)
Founder members: K. Alabyan, V. Babenkov, V. Baburov, A. Vlasov, F. Deryabin, N. Zapletin, A. Zaslavsky, A. Zilpert, K. Ivanov, G. Kozelkov, G. Kochar, F. Krestin, M. Kryakov, M. Kupovsky, M. Mazmanyan, I. Matsa, A. Mikhailov, A. Mordvinnov, N. Poliakov, G. Terekhin, V. Simbirtsev, Slodovnik, A. Faifel
President: I. Matsa
Vice-president: A. Zaslavsky
Secretary: V. Baburov

Management: G. Kozelkov, A. Mordinov, B. Simbirtsev, F. Deryabin
Sections established in Leningrad, Tomsk, in the Ukraine and Georgia
Section in Erivan for Armenian affairs with K. Alabyan, G. Kochar, M. Mazmanian, A. Aragonian, O. Makarian

VANO Moscow 1930–2
(Scientific All-union Association of Architecture)
Consisted of ASNOVA, ARU and OSA (SASS). In Moscow known as MOVANO
Bureau for the organization run by Aslanov
Presidents: 1930 – K. Dzhus; 1931 – N. Voronkov; 1932 – V. Markov
Productivity: N. Selivanov
Secretary: Yu. Savitsky

UNION OF THE ARCHITECTS OF THE USSR
18 May 1932
Management: K. Alabyan, V. Balikhin, S. Babaev, M. Ginsburg, I. Zholtovsky, A. Zaslavsky, M. Kryukov, N. Ladovsky, V. Markov, A. Urban, D. Fridman
President of the builders: E. Kelin
28 October 1932 Preparation for an all-union congress
Organizing committee: K. Alabyan, A. Aleksandrov, D. Arkin, G. Barkhin, L. Bumazhny, V. Vesnin, M. Ginsburg, I. Zholtovsky, A. Zaslavsky, B. Iofan, N. Kolli, M. Kryukov, A. Mordinov, L. Perchik, I. Fomin, D. Fridman, S. Chernyshev, A. Shchusev, N. Kosumov, N. Langebard, A. Nikolsky, F. Simonov, N. Khomutetsky, V. Shchuko, P. Aleshin, I. Mashkov, M. Kholostenko, I. Shafran, Ya. Shteinberg, G. Kochar, E. Mamedov, D. Ivanishvili, A. Voinov, B. Oserov, P. Volodin
Praesidium of the committee: A. Alabyan, A. Aleksandrov, V. Vesnin, I. Zholotovsky, B. Iofan, N. Kolli, M. Kryukov, S. Chernyshev, I. Shafran, V. Shchuko, A. Shchusev
Secretaries of the organizing committee: K. Alabyan, A. Aleksandrov, I. Zholtovsky, N. Kolli, M. Krukov

The First Congress of Soviet Architects was held in Moscow 16–26 June 1937

285

285 Iofan, Gelfreich and Roudner: Palace of the Soviets, 1932, final premiated design which marked the end of the first phase of the modern movement in Russia and set the pattern for the officially approved architecture that was to follow.

418 Soviet delegates and a thousand guests from different parts of the country

Various countries from abroad were represented

Czechoslovakia – I. Gochar

Rumania – P. Janek

Great Britain – B. Garrett

Belgium – A. Vervek

USA – Frank Lloyd Wright

Turkey – A. Burkhan

as well as delegates from Spain, France, Sweden, Norway and Denmark

Reports on Soviet architecture by K. Alabyan, N. Kolli, A. Shchusev

Reports by various Soviet republics and S. Chernyshev and L. Ilyin on the planning and reconstruction of towns

B. Iofan, V. Shchuko, V. Gelfreich on the Palace of Councils

M. Ginsburg on the industrialization of housing

M. Kryukov on the teaching of architecture

I. Zholtovsky on the education of an architect

A. Zaslavsky on the Statute of Soviet Architects

Elected administration

Responsible executive secretary: K. Alabyan

Secretary for education: D. Arkin

Secretary for the organization: V. Dedukhin

Members of the praesidium: A. Bulushev, B. Iofan, N. Kolli, A. Mordinov, S. Chernyshev, D. Chechulin, G. Golovko

Administrators: N. Bunyatian, V. Vesnin, M. Ginsburg, P. Golovchenko, S. Dadashev, A. Hegello, L. Ilyin, V. Kussakov, A. Kryachkov, A. Molokin, I. Zholtovsky, A. Zaslavsky, A. Ivanishvili, G. Paklin, L. Rudnev, F. Steblin, A. Chevchetko, S. Grigoriev, G. Kochar, M. Kryukov, G. Ludwig, M. Mazmanyan, N. Baranov, P. Kvartirnikov, P. Trestling, A. Bessolov, L. Bumazhny, V. Golli, S. Novikov, P. Potskhishvili, B. Rubanenko, G. Simonov, H. Tairova, I. Fomin, Ya. Shteinberg, A. Dukelsky, G. Mamedov, V. Mukhamedov

Candidate members of the administration: B. Kalimullin, Y. Kornfeld, V. Kuznetsov, A. Kurdyani, M. Usseinov

Inspection commission: V. Altschuler, A. Vlassov, I. Valeev, M. Sakhautdinov, M. Tomakh, A. Sharov

Candidate member of the inspection commission: S. Georgeeva

The Statute of the Union of Architects of the USSR was ratified on 23 August 1937 by the Sovnarkom (People's Council of the USSR)

Bibliography

1916   Malevich, K. *Ot Kubizma i Futurizma k Suprematizmu* (in Russian, *From Cubism and Futurism to Suprematism*) Moscow

1919   Malevich, K. *O Novykh Sistemakh v Iskusstve* (in Russian, *of New System in Art*) Vitebsk

1920   Malevich, K. *Ot Sezanna do Suprematizma* (in Russian, *From Cezanne to Suprematism*) Moscow

1921   Punin, N. *Protiv Kubizma. Tatlin* (*Against Cubism. Tatlin*). Petersburg.

       Gallerie Der Sturm, Berlin *Austellung Puni* (exhibition catalogue)

1922   E. Lissitzky The *Story of Two Squares* De Stijl

       Ehrenburg, I. 'Ein Entwurf Tatlins' *Fruhlicht* March 1922

       Réau, L. *L'Art Russe – De Pierre Le Grand à nos Jours* Vol II, Paris

       Carter, H. 'Rebuilding Soviet Russia' series of articles in Vol 56 of *The Architects' Journal* (p. 336 ff; p. 373 ff; p. 408 ff; p. 438 ff; p. 473 ff; p. 610 ff; p. 645 ff)

1924   Kallai, E. *Konstruktivismus* Jahrbuch Der Jungen Kunst, Leipzig

       El Lissitzky 'Element Und Erfindung' *ABC* January

1925   'Exposition International des Arts Décoratifs et Industriels Modernes, URSS' (catalogue) Musée des Arts Décoratifs, Paris

       El Lissitzky and Hans Arp *Kunstismen 1914–1924* Zurich

       El Lissitzky 'Architektur Der SSSR' *Kunstblatt* February

1926   Mendelsohn, E. *Russland – Europa – Amerika* Berlin

       'Oltargavsky' *American Architect* vol. 130 pp. 210–15

       Auffray, P. 'Architectures soviétiques' *Cahiers D'Art* p. 103

1927   Malewitsch, K. *Die Gegenstandslose Welt* Bauhausbücher, vol. XI, Munich

       'Nouvelles Architectures Sovietiques' p. 40 *Cahiers D'Art* p. 40

       Taut, B. *Ein Wohnhaus* Stuttgart

       Fülop-Miller, R. *The Mind and Face of Bolshevism* London

       'Mansurov' (exhibition catalogue) Museum of Pictorial Culture, Leningrad

1928   'Katalog Der Sowiet-Pavillons Auf Der Internationalen Presse-Austellung' (exhibition catalogue) Cologne

'Mansurov' (exhibition catalogue) Galleria Bragaglia, Rome

Barkine, G. 'Architecture Russe' *Cahiers de Belgique* p. 228

Baldovici, J. 'L'Architecture russe en URSS' *L'Architecture vivante* vol. 1, Paris

1929 Taut, B. *Modern Architecture* London (and Stuttgart)

'Les Dernières Réalisations architecturales en Russie' *Cahiers d'Art* vol IV pp. 47–50 illustrated

Barr, A. H. 'Notes on Russian Architecture' *The Arts* 1929 no. I, p. 103

1930 El Lissitzky *Russland, Die Rekonstruktion Der Architektur in Der Sowjetunion* Coll. Neues Bauten in Der Welt, Joseph Gantner, vol. I, Vienna (Schroll)

Tischold, J. 'El Lissitzky' *Imprimatur* III

Margold, J. E. *Bauten Der Volkserziehung und Volksgesundheit* Berlin

Baldovici, J. 'Le Moment Architectural En URSS' *L'Architecture Vivante* vol. II

1931 'Le Palais de la Culture à Léningrad' *Cahiers D'Art* p. 384

1932 Woznicki, S. T. 'USSR – On Problems of Architecture' *T-Square* vol. II (Nov.) pp. 80–83 illustrated

Byron, R. and B. Lubetkin, 'The Russian Scene' *The Architectural Review* (May) vol. 71 pp. 173–214 illustrated

Special issue of *L'Architecture d'Aujourd'hui* November 1932 includes essays by G. Mequet, G. Sebilie, A. Agache, P. Monteiro, J. J. Coulon, C. Dedoyard, P. M. Bardi, G. H. Pingusson

1933 Woznicki, S. T. 'The Style of Future Soviet Architecture' *Architektura; Budownietwo* vol. 9 pp. 270–75

Baldovici, J. 'Salles de Spectacle, Le moment héroïque de l'architecture moderne en URSS' *L'Architecture Vivante* vol. III, Paris

'Tendances d'architecture en URSS' *Formes* no. 32

Loukomski, G. K. 'Il Ritorno Dell'Architettura Classica in Russia' *Rassegna Di Architettura* p. 175

1934 Piacentini, M. 'Un Grande Avvenimento Architettonico in Russia. Il Palazzo Dei Soviet A Mosca' *Architettura* March

Lurcat, A. 'Architecture en URSS' *Art Vivant* p. 161

Rocco, G. 'Ritorni classici nell'architettura russa' *Rassegna di Architettura* p. 183

Drahomanov S. 'L'Enseignement de l'Urbanisms en URSS' *Urbanisme* p. 334

1935   Voice, A. 'Contemporary Soviet Architecture' *American Magazine of Art* vol. 28, pp. 527–35

Maigrot, E. 'L'Urbanisme et L'Architecture en URSS' *L'Architecture* p. 449

Schwan, B. *Stadtbau Und Wohnungswesen Der Welt* Berlin

Midana, A. 'Nota Sull'Architettura E L'Edilizia Dell' URSS' *L'Architettura Italiana* October

Arkin, D. 'Architecture' *The Studio* special volume dedicated to 'Art in the USSR'

Rocco, G. 'Architettura dell' URSS' *Rassegna di Architettura* p. 313

1936   Fariello, E. 'L'Urbanistica e L'Abitazione in Russia' *Architettura* September

1937   Wright, F. L. 'Architecture and Life in USSR' *Architectural Record* October

Rubenstein, A. 'Nouvelle Architecture ou retour au passé ?'

Breines, S. 'First Congress of Soviet Architects' *Architectural Record* October

Trotsky, N. A. 'The House of the Soviets in Leningrad' *Arkhitektura Leningrada* vol. 2 pp. 8–12.

1940   Alekseev B. 'Novoe v Tvorchestvo V. E. Tatlina' *Tvorchestvo* no. 8 pp. 14–15

1942   Blumenfeld, H. 'Regional and City Planning in the Soviet Union' *Task* October

Meyer, H. 'El Arquitecto Sovietico' *Arquitectura* Mexico City, no. 9 pp. 3–19

'Soviet Architecture' *Task* no. 3 pp. 24–32

Vesnin, V. 'Anglo-Soviet Bonds in Architecture' *RIBA Journal* vol. 49 p. 164

Carter, E. 'Soviet Architecture Today' *Architectural Review* vol. 92 pp. 107–14

1943   Kolly, N. 'Organisation of Reconstruction in USSR' *RIBA Journal* vol. 51 pp. 40–41

Percival, D. 'Soviet Architects' *Plan* no. 1, pp. 11–12

1944   Krasilnikov, V. 'Cablegram from Russia . . .' *Architects' Journal* vol. 100 p. 210

'Socialist Realism' *Architectural Review* vol. 95 p. 24

'Soviet Architecture Today' *Task* (winter 1944–45) pp. 37–45

Arkin, D. 'La Arquitectura En Rusia Y La Guerra' *Arquitectura* August, Mexico City

1945   Kouznetsov 'Crise du Logement et Reconstruction en URSS' *Architecture d'Aujourd'hui* July–August pp. 47–49

Hamlin, T. 'The Development of Russian Architecture' *Magazine of Art* vol. 38

1946 'How Building and Planning are Organised in the USSR' *Architects' Journal* vol. 104 pp. 79–86

Bunt, C. G. E. *Russian Art from Scythes to Soviets* The Studio, London and New York

1948 'Constructivism' *Art News* vol. 47 pp. 22–25

Sartoris, A. *Encyclopédie De L'Architecture Nouvelle Ordre Et Climat Nordiques* Milan

Voice, A. *Russian Architecture* Philosophical Library, New York

1949 Moholy-Nagy, Laszlo *The New Vision* New York

1950 Seuphor, M. 'Suprématisme et Néoplasticisme' *Art d'Aujourd'hui* no. 7–8 March

1952 Gabo, N. 'On Constructive Realism' *Architects' Yearbook*

1953 Alvard, J. 'Les Idées de Malevitch' *Art d'Aujourd'hui* no. 5 July

1955 Habasque, G. 'Documents Inédits Sur les débuts de Suprématisme' *Aujourd'hui: art and architecture* no. 4 September

Suephor, M. 'An temps de l'avant-garde. L'Architecture en URSS' *L'Oeil* special number dedicated to 'L'Art en Russie'

1957 Bourgeois, V. 'Salut au Constructivisme' *Zodiac* no. 1

'La Grandiosa rivoluzione culturale realizzata in URSS dell' ottobre ad oggi' *Rinascita* November

1958 Richter, H. *El Lissitzky* Cologne

Ripellino, A. M. *Il Cubofuturismo Russo* Conferenza alla Galleria Nazionale d'Arte Moderna, Rome

1959 Gray, C. *Lissitzky* (exhibition catalogue), Whitechapel Art Gallery, London

Gray, C. *Malevich* (exhibition catalogue), Whitechapel Art Gallery, London

Ripellino, A. M. *Majakovski E Il Teatro Russo D'Avanguardio* Turin

1960 Gray, C. 'Lissitzky, Typographer' *Typographica* (New Series)

'Architettura Suprematista di Kasimir Malevitsch' *L' Architettura* September

Banham, R. *Theory and Design in the First Machine Age* London

1962   Conrads and Sperlich *Fantastic Architecture* G and C. C.
       Collins, London
      Gray, C. 'Rodchenko: Constructivist designer' *Portfolio*
       New York and London
      Cray, C. *The Great Experiment* London
      Casabella-Continuità no. 262, April. Dedicated to the USSR
      'Panorama dell' edilizia residenziale in URSS' *Casabella-*
       Continuità no. 263 May
1963   de Feo, V. *URSS Architettura 1917–1936* Editori Riuniti
1965   Marshall, H. *Mayakovsky* London
1967   Kopp, A. *Ville et Revolution* Paris; English edition, London
       1970
1968   Kueppers-Lissitzky, S. *El Lissitzky* London
      Hill, A. *Data* London
      Malevich, K. *Essays on Art* 2 vols. Copenhagen (English
       translation)
1969   Starr, F. 'Melnikov' *Architectural Design* (*AD*), July
      'Poetry Must be made by All' (exhibition Catalogue)
       Moderna Museet, Stockholm
1970   'Constructivist Architecture in the USSR' *Architectural*
      Design (*AD*) February (special number)

Index

Numbers in italics refer to illustrations